PLANTATIONS and DEATH CAMPS

innovations
African American religious thought

Anthony B. Pinn and Katie G. Cannon, editors

Innovations publishes creative and innovative works in African American religious thought and experience. The series highlights creatively progressive projects in Womanist and Black theology and ethics. It also encourages interdisciplinary discourse that expands understanding of African American religion and religious experience as well as the manner in which African Americans have envisioned and articulated their religiosity.

Titles in the series—

Enfleshing Freedom: Body, Race, and Being
M. Shawn Copeland

Creative Exchange: A Constructive Theology
of African American Religious Experience
Victor Anderson

Making a Way Out of No Way: A Womanist Theology
Monica A. Coleman

Plantations and Death Camps: Race, Sin, and Human Dignity
Beverly Eileen Mitchell

PLANTATIONS and DEATH CAMPS

Religion, Ideology, and Human Dignity

BEVERLY EILEEN MITCHELL

Fortress Press

Minneapolis

This book is dedicated to the men and women
who served on plantations, labor and death camps;
and to the children who could not

Cover art: Electric Fence © Krzysztof Dydynski/Lonely Planet Images/Getty Images; Child Victim © Janek Skarzynski/AFP/Getty Images; Man © American School/Getty Images; and Slave Cabins © Blaine Harrington/Corbis.
Cover design: Laurie Ingram
Book design: PerfecType, Nashville, Tenn.

Mitchell, Beverly Eileen.
   Plantations and death camps : religion, ideology, and human dignity / by Beverly Eileen Mitchell.
      p. cm. — (Innovations : African American religious thought)
   Includes bibliographical references and index.
   ISBN 978-0-8006-6330-8 (alk. paper)
   1. Dignity—Religious aspects—Christianity. 2. Slavery. 3. Holocaust, Jewish (1939-1945) 4. Racism—Religious aspects—Christianity. I. Title.
   BT702.M58 2009
   261.8'3315—dc22
                                   2008036837
The paper used in this publication meets the minimum requirements of American National Standard for Information Sciences—Permanence of Paper for Printed Library Materials, ANSI Z329.48-1984.

Manufactured in the U.S.A.

CONTENTS

PREFACE

At first glance, black slavery and the Jewish Holocaust seem to have little in common. The hapless victims of slave plantations were exploited for their labor, whereas Jews and others deemed undesirable were sent to labor camps and death camps. White supremacy and anti-Semitism involved two distinct populations and had different historical trajectories. Nevertheless, despite the seeming incongruence of looking at black slavery and the Jewish Holocaust together, a side-by-side examination does offer important insights into what it means to be human. This study demonstrates that black slavery and the Jewish Holocaust reveal a common humanity in which human dignity and human deface- ment are *both* theological and political realities.

In developing this central thesis, *Plantations and Death Camps: Religion, Ideology, and Human Dignity* unmasks a startling reality regarding the nature of human dignity in the context of sordid degradation. The sight of black slaves working on large and small plantations or displayed on auction blocks as if they were mere livestock does not immediately conjure up a picture of dignity and worth. Nor does the sight of emaciated men and women with tattered clothes in an unsanitary hovel of a death camp evoke the glory and majesty of human beings made in the image of God. Nevertheless, I argue that it is *precisely* on the plantations, in the ghettos, and in the death camps that the dignity of the human being *can* and *must* be affirmed, despite all appearances to the contrary.

This volume provides a Judeo-Christian foundation for understanding what it means to be human in light of the challenges men, women, and children have encountered in the past and will face in the twenty-first century. I contend that reflection on what it means to be human cannot be rightly understood in the abstract. Because we human beings are not representations of an abstract concept of humanity but people with historical experiences and social locations, theological reflection on what it means to be human must be carried out with concrete individuals and specific communities in mind. With the record of the lives of men, women, and youth—in the form of diaries, journals, memoirs, and oral histories—serving as a backdrop for theological reflection, such abstract concepts as the *imago Dei*, human dignity, sin, and idolatry become concrete in flesh and blood. These concepts have been informed by the experience of those who once lived, suffered unjustly, and sometimes died in the midst of struggle against human evil in the good creation.

This volume documents what happens when members of societies fail to safeguard and protect the dignity and worth of every member. My hope is that this examination of the historical experiences of blacks in slavery and of Jews in the Holocaust will lead all people of good will to become more alert to their own attitudes and beliefs that could contribute to the dehumanization of others. Our failure to protect the dignity of all in our societies will make acts of dehumanization, oppression, and human slaughter easier to perpetrate.

With these concerns in mind, in chapter 1—through slave narratives and oral testimonies of former slaves and through diaries of Jewish victims and memoirs of Holocaust survivors—I identify the common features of these two groups' respective experiences and justify why human dignity can be affirmed even in extreme situations of degradation. In chapter 2, I articulate the theological basis for what it means to be human and I maintain that human dignity is the glory of the image of God in humanity. I also provide a comprehensive definition of the sin of dehumanization, which I call "defacement." In chapter 3, I trace the development of black antipathy and anti-Judaism as communal forms of defacement beginning in the ancient world and on through modernity. In chapter 4, I establish that certain tenets of Western philosophical thought in modernity provided the intellectual support for racialism—the shared link between white supremacy and anti-Semitism.

In chapter 5, I articulate the ways in which white supremacy and anti-Semitism, as forms of communal defacement, functioned as ideologies of death, and I demonstrate that the theological root of both of these ideologies is idolatry. Finally, in chapter 6, I maintain that theological reflection on human dignity and defacement is incomplete unless it leads to the kind of transformation that can facilitate change in society. I contend that if slavery and the Holocaust reveal a common humanity in which human dignity and defacement are theological and political realities, then this revelation demands the kind of conversion and commitment in which our personal and communal lives, as well as our social structures and systems, are oriented toward protecting human dignity, especially that of the marginalized.

■ ■ ■

I am grateful to Wesley Theological Seminary for the sabbatical that gave me the time to devote to this project in fall 2005. In particular, I would like to thank Bruce C. Birch, academic dean, for his interest and encouragement. I am also grateful to the faculty of Wesley Theological Seminary for their continued support and interest in my work. In particular, I want to express my appreciation to Joseph Tortorici, who provided me with material on human dignity in the Roman Catholic tradition. I am deeply indebted to Howertine Farrell Duncan, research librarian at Wesley Theological Seminary, for her assistance in obtaining interlibrary loans for pertinent books and articles. Her expertise, thoughtfulness, and ready assistance were invaluable. I would also like to thank Quentin Graham for his wise counsel and listening ear along the way.

I also wish to extend my thanks to Michael West for his vision for this book as well as Susan Johnson and Carolyn Banks for their work in bringing this book to print.

I am most appreciative of the love and support of my family. In particular, I am grateful to my parents, Marvin and Edwina Mitchell, for their continued prayers and encouragement. I also thank my sisters, Joyce and Janice, for helping me to "keep it real!"

Dignity in the Shadow Side of Human Experience

Our life was a misery.

—JACK MADDOX

Our life is a life of helpless terror.

—YITSKHOK RUDASHEVSKI

There can be no stranger notion to ponder than the juxtaposition of images of slave plantations and death camps with the concept of human dignity. Raw welts caused by a lash snapping across glistening black skin do not evoke the image of human dignity. Nor does the hollow-eyed, pale face of a meagerly clothed adult male, emaciated by the unintentional loss of 70 pounds from a 160-pound frame, evoke a sense of well-being and optimism for the fulfillment of human potential. What connects these two disparate images, along with many other horrifying images from the closing years of the twentieth century, is that each reflects the plight of a human being forced to endure degradation at the hands of fellow human beings. Like death, the violation of a person's dignity is a great leveler. The violent assault on the dignity of a human being is a terrible wound to the spirit whether one is of African or European descent, a Gentile or a Jew, or born a slave or free. The inner cry of revolt against dehumanization in such situations bears witness to a *common* humanity.

The notion of a common humanity runs counter to the prevailing trend in contemporary theology in which it is fashionable for various constituencies of the theological community to emphasize diversity and to particularize the theological concerns that arise out of a specific set of economic, social, and political realities. This focus on particularity has been a counterresponse to long-standing tendencies in theological reflection to posit a form of universalism that obscured diversity and masked imperialistic pretensions toward the disinherited. The attempt to avoid co-optation from the dominant culture is an important act of resistance. However, in an age in which we see frequent attempts by conflicting parties to demonize their opponents and to unleash acts of savagery without impunity, I believe it is imperative that we affirm our *common* humanity often, even as we celebrate our respective differences with members of other ethnic, social, economic, and political communities. The urgency that accompanies this appeal to affirm a common humanity arises out of a recognition that the first step toward the kind of atrocities perpetrated against hapless groups, historically, is invariably made when we forget the commonalities that bind us together as members of one human family. Once we no longer see ourselves as fellow human beings with a shared capacity for joy and profound sadness, for pleasure and immense pain, for exaltation and great suffering, then it is easy to take the subsequent steps that lead to mistreatment, brutality, degradation, and attempted destruction of one another.

Commonalities of *human* experience bind the victims of black slavery and the Jewish Holocaust. These commonalities are worth exploring, for they show poignantly and graphically what it means to be human and how it feels to have the sacredness of one's humanity scorned or even denied. In the following discussion, I make no attempt to obscure the distinctions that separate the black experience of slavery and its aftermath in North America from the Jewish experience of the Nazi attempt to systematically exterminate European Jewry. The distinctions in those particular experiences of oppression are important to preserve because each story holds dimensions of uniqueness. Nevertheless, the commonalities that bind the black community and the Jewish community as members of the human family are just as important, for they reveal key elements about the nature of what it means to be a human creature in the sight of God.

The Atlantic slave trade, the exploitation inherent in plantation life, the terror of the Ku Klux Klan, and the myriad of humiliations wrought through segregation, permeating every facet of black life, brought their own distinctive experiences of horror and misery. Likewise, the escalation of harassment, the ruthless dispossession, the frequent seasons of senseless persecution, and the "final solution" brought their own reign of terror to the Jews. While it is true that black slavery and the Holocaust were historical occurrences arising from different contexts, the narratives and memoirs of the survivors indicate that they inhabited very similar psychic and emotional terrain. It is through the responses to degradation that we can find some common ground. Neither blacks nor Jews were an amorphous group of abstract "humanity" but, rather, were flesh-and-blood men, women, and even children, who felt, suffered, and died under state-sponsored systems of oppression and attempts to annihilate the soul as well as the body. Each group knew what it meant to have its dignity assaulted.

Philosopher Simone Weil once said that the most significant dimension of human dignity is that each of us carries within us a visceral response to the experience of having our humanity denied or our dignity assaulted.[1] I believe that this universal recoil from a denial of our dignity, and the suffering that accompanies that denial, is a crucial element in defining what it means to be a human being. This aspect of being human is present in poignant, visceral, and dramatic ways in the narratives of former black slaves as well as the memoirs of Holocaust survivors. But immediately, the question arises: How can we speak about human dignity in the context of black slavery and the Jewish Shoah?[2] The answer lies in this assertion: *The dignity of being a human made in the image of God was manifested* precisely *in the bearing witness of the violations and in the protest against those violations, whether the assaults were physical, emotional, or spiritual.*

Several common features of Jewish persecution and black oppression provide useful parallels that support the assertion that the indestructible character of human dignity can be seen concretely in the inner, soulful cry of protest of blacks and Jews in the face of deliberate, systematic attempts to deny their full humanity. Among the common features of Jewish and black oppression are forced segregation from the larger society; familial separations; physical, emotional, and spiritual deprivations; the brutality of oppressors; the outrage of degradation; and the need to bear witness against dehumanizing conditions. Other common features of their experience are also worth noting in conjunction with those identified above, including the particularity of women's suffering, the agonizing transports to their place of subjugation, and the special humiliations found in being forced to dwell in one's own filth. In the rest of this chapter, men, women, and children who suffered under black slavery or the Jewish Holocaust will bear witness to the violation of their human dignity in their own words.

Set Apart as Pariahs

The forced separation of one group from others within society is a common tactic of systematic dehumanization of a designated "pariah" group. Such a designation has often circumscribed the movement of persons associated with the pariah group. They are denied access to certain places and to services associated with full membership in society. Persons so designated have often been forced to carry "official" identification of their status or to wear particular clothes or other markings that make it easier to spot their existence. The "pariah factor" makes it easier for others in society to see the pariah group as less than human, and any maltreatment directed against that group will be seen as justified. This in turn also makes it easier for others in society to perpetuate the customs that help maintain the pariah status.

With Adolf Hitler's rise to power in the early 1930s, and the establishment of National Socialism as the political foundation for Nazism, Jews were forced to relinquish their full participation in German society. As Hitler came to power, the Jews' opportunities narrowed and their movement in society was limited. Their comings and goings were prescribed in ways that set them apart and made them feel alienated from the rest of society. In 1938, a

young writer, fourteen-year-old Klaus Lager, recalled the observation of "the day of National Solidarity." Jews were not permitted
to go outdoors from noon until eight in the evening. He recalls
that they were also ordered to carry photo identity cards. They
were not permitted to own driver's licenses. At the same time,
in Berlin, Lager observed: "Jews are no longer allowed to live or
walk on certain streets, usually along the grand avenues."[3] After
he escaped to Denmark the following year, Lager noted omi-
nously: "To be in a war in Germany as a Jew means to be ready
for the worst."[4] For the Jews in Germany like Lager, segregation
from mainstream society was an initial step toward the eventual
attempt to annihilate them.

Segregation from mainstream society was a hallmark of the
experience of African Americans in the United States, beginning
from slavery. W. B. Allen, a black minister, noted the degree to
which slaves had little control over their movements and activities: "The plantation rules forbade a slave to: own a firearm, leave
home without a pass, sell or buy anything without his master's
consent, have a light in his cabin after a certain hour at night,
attend any secret meeting, harbor or in any manner assist a runaway slave, abuse a farm animal, mistreat a member of his family . . . and a great many other things."[5] Part of the pariah factor
included the exclusion of black slaves from educational opportunities. Former slave Hal Hutson recalls what it was like when he
tried to learn how to read and to do mathematics. "If I was caught
trying to read or figger, dey would whip me something terrible."[6]
Anna Lee recalls the scorn of whites at the prospect of blacks
seeking to educate themselves: "No sir, the white people, they did
not try to help me learn to read and write; said they did not have
time to fool with us, as we were too thick-headed to ever learn

anything."[7] Meanwhile, quasi-free blacks in the North, prior to the Civil War, came to experience the limitations placed on their movement in society. In the years following the emancipation of the slaves and the failure of Reconstruction, well into the twentieth century blacks both in the North and especially in the South came to know firsthand the dehumanizing practice of Jim Crow.

One elderly Jewish man who escaped from Germany as a teenager lived to articulate the similarities between the experience of segregation of the Jews in Germany and that of segregation of African Americans in the southern United States before the civil rights movement. At a symposium at the United States Holocaust Memorial Museum in Washington, D.C., a few years ago, Georg Iggers recalled his experience of moving to the southern United States in 1938: "I moved to Richmond, Virginia, while still in high school. I saw how the blacks were treated there. They were being treated just like we Jews were being treated in Germany."[8] To Iggers, the treatment of blacks—segregated into substandard housing, forced to use separate and *un*equal public facilities, subject to demeaning treatment from whites of any class, and presumed inferior on the basis of skin color—evoked obvious, unmistakable parallels to his own experience and that of fellow Jews in Nazi Germany in 1938. The sense of shame and humiliation that the Jews of Germany and the blacks of the United States felt were similar, even though the contexts for their separation were different. Blacks were made to feel shame and humiliation because they were treated as incapable of assuming responsibility for their own self-determination. Jews were made to feel shame and humiliation because they were treated as undesirables. For both groups, the pariah factor was a blow to their dignity and sense of self-worth.

Wrenching Familial Separations

In addition to sharing the humiliating pariah factor, black slaves and Jews also shared the wrenching experience of forced separation from family members. During both black slavery and Jewish internment in labor and concentration camps, mothers were frequently separated from their children, husbands from their wives, and siblings from one another. Mary Reynolds, a former slave, recalled the trauma of those familial separations on the slave plantations in America. She told an interviewer: "I seen chillum sold off and de mammy not sold, and sometimes de mammy sold and a little baby kept on de place and give to another woman to raise."[9] For Mary and countless others, the painfulness of such scenes was heightened because the slaveholders never seemed to recognize how devastating those experiences were to the slaves. She continued: "Dem white folks didn't care nothing 'bout how de slaves grieved when dey tore up a family."[10] Stephen Williams, also a former slave, commented on the phenomenon many years after he had observed such scenes as a small child:

> Man, man, folks what didn't go through slavery ain't got no idea what it was. . . . I was jus' a little chap, like I've told you, but I can remember that place like it happened yesterday—husbands sold away from wives, and children taken away from mothers. A trader, them days, didn't think no more of selling a baby or little child away from its mother than taking a little calf away from a cow.[11]

Charles Ball, also a former slave from Maryland, observed in his slave narrative that his parents were owned by different slaveholders and that his mother was taken away from her children and sold to a new owner in Georgia. Subsequently, the children were all sold to different owners in the area. Ball reports that his father never recovered from the loss of his wife and family to the slave system.[12] In an equally poignant recollection, Kate Drumgoold recalled many years after the fact the trauma of being permanently separated from her mother, who was sold to an owner from Georgia:

> My mother was sold . . . and we did not know that she was
> sold until she was gone. . . . I used to go outside and look up
> to see if there was anything that would direct me, and I saw
> a clear place in the sky, and it seemed to me the way she had
> gone, and *I watched it three and a half years*, not knowing what
> that meant, and it was there the whole time that mother was
> gone from her little ones.[13]

Familial separation was also an important part of the experience of the deported Jews' journey into the "kingdom of night." In *Five Chimneys*, Olga Lengyel, guilt-ridden and haunted, shared her experience of having made decisions that she believed ultimately led to the deaths of her elderly parents and her two sons—all in a bid to keep her family together when her husband was notified that he was to be transported. She opens her memoir with the following "confession":

> *Mea culpa*, my fault, *mea maxima culpa*! I cannot acquit myself
> of the charge that I am, in part, responsible for the destruc-
> tion of my own parents and of my two young sons. The world
> understands that I could not have known, but in my heart the
> terrible feeling persists that I could have, I might have, saved
> them.[14]

After Lengyel's entire family arrived at Auschwitz, the "selection" process began. Her father and husband were immediately separated from the rest of the family. Her younger son, Thomas, was classed with the other small children and the elderly—all of which were "selected" for immediate execution. Because Lengyel sought to spare her older son, Arvad, from hard work, he was also classed with the small children and elderly. Completely unaware of their fate, she persuaded the chief selector to permit her mother to go with her two sons. Later she found out the devastating truth. She wrote in her memoir: "How could I have known? I had spared them from hard work, but I had condemned Arvad and my mother to death in the gas chambers."[15]

Another Jewish survivor recalls the lasting pain of abrupt separation from a parent at Auschwitz:

> I arrived with my mother to Auschwitz. It was night and the lights, and the dogs, and the screaming. . . . I was frightened. My mother kept stroking my face, "Don't worry, we will be okay. Don't worry, we will be okay." And it only took a few moments and she was gone. I ran after her screaming, "Mother! Mother! . . . and she reached out her arms with a bewildered look. . . . I can never forget that look.[16]

This survivor never saw her mother again.

Well-known Italian writer Primo Levi also wrote about the familial separations he observed as a concentration camp inmate. Not only were those separations wrenching, but he was struck, perhaps even more, by the callousness of the guards who greeted each new shipment of doomed Jews with remorseless deception. In *Survival in Auschwitz*, Levi writes: "Someone dared to ask for his luggage: they replied, 'luggage afterwards'. Someone else did not want to leave his wife: they said, 'together again afterwards'. Many mothers did not want to be separated from their children: They said 'good, good, stay with the child.' They [the camp guards] behaved with the calm assurance of people doing their normal duty of every day."[17] Of course, the false assurances of the guards were meant to pacify the anxious Jews, who would learn too late the truth of what would become of them and their loved ones.

Neither those who devised institutional instructions that dictated familial separation nor those charged with the responsibility for carrying them out could ever have executed those orders without a bad conscience had they truly believed that a Jewish mother or a black slave mother had the capacity to grieve as deeply as they themselves could. The absence of empathetic imagination—the inability to see members of the "pariah" group as being like oneself—is the psychological foundation for participation in dehumanizing a fellow human being. Although the anguished cries of the mothers and fathers and of the children served as the protest against such attempts at dehumanization, the hearts of many camp guards and slaveholders, like the ancient pharaoh of Egypt, were hardened.

The Humiliation of Deprivations

Another shared experience of enslaved blacks and Jewish internees was the humiliation of having basic physical, emotional, and spiritual needs denied. In their respective contexts, blacks and Jews shared both minor and major privations that defined life for black slaves on the slave plantation and contributed to the death of Jews in the internment camps. When those men and women were reduced to scratching desperately for their daily bread, for raiment to protect their bodies, and for a decent place to shelter themselves from the elements, it was difficult for even them to view themselves as creatures of dignity and worth.

Many years after her emancipation from slavery, Louisa Adams could still recall not only the intensity of hunger that gnawed at her but also the sense of moral guilt she experienced when she felt forced to steal food to survive. Years after her emancipation, Adams stated rather baldly to an interviewer: "We were so hungry we were bound to steal or perish."[18] She described her own theft of food as a "breach of morality." But if her actions are judged as a "breach of morality," they are completely dwarfed by the brutality inherent in the inhumane system that robbed Adams and thousands of other slaves of their liberty. Another former slave, Jacob Manson, recalled that same level of hunger and noted the undignified scramble for a morsel to eat: "We had poor food, an' de young slaves wus fed outen troughs. De food was put in a trough an' de little niggers[19] gathered round an' et."[20] Other ex-slaves also reflected on the fact that meeting basic needs for survival sometimes meant disregarding the biblical injunction against theft.

Not all slaves were troubled by their consciences when it came to stealing food from their masters. In his slave narrative, Lewis Clarke maintained that "in view of the sufferings of this day, we felt fully justified in making a foraging expedition upon the milkroom [at] night."[21] Clarke actually cataloged the items he stole. He explained: "This [act of stealing] was not malice in us; we did not love the waste which the hogs made; but we must have something to eat, to pay for the cruel and reluctant fast; and when we had obtained this, we must of course cover up our tracks."[22] Although the slaves were watched closely, the temptation to steal came from their hunger, which they felt compelled to satisfy even if it rendered them as thieves.[23] Moreover, Clarke observed, "White folks stole all the days of [our] lives; what was immoral among the slaves was stealing from *each other*."[24]

Not all slaves were as ill fed as Lewis Clarke and Louisa Adams, but for those Jews in the labor and death camps, the tale of insatiable hunger that gripped many of them is legendary. Author Aaron Hass noted that, for most survivors, the Holocaust was "a thousand days of hunger, a thousand daydreams of food (a commodity worth countless gambles with one's life.)"[25] The scramble for food could reduce the most cultured camp internee to the status of a groveling creature. As Hass wrote in *The Aftermath*, one Jewish woman recalled the fights for food in the camps as follows:

> We had to fight for everything in Majdanek: for a scrap of floor space in the hut on which to stretch out at night, for a rusty bowl without with we could not obtain the miserable ration of nettle soup which they fed us, of yellowing stinking water to drink. . . . Fear and horror overcame me at the sight of women prisoners struggling over a scrap of free space on the floor, or hitting one another over the head at the soup kettles, snatching bowls.[26]

Olga Lengyel, a camp inmate previously mentioned, observed a similar, almost vicious, animal-like scramble for the most meager of rations at Auschwitz. She wrote: "For, seeing the kettle, some women were never able to control themselves, and fell upon the food like animals in a death struggle."[27] Noted Austrian psychiatrist Viktor Frankl, also a Holocaust survivor, wrote of the importance of food for the prisoners as he recalled the ration of a five-ounce piece of bread as their only food in four days. In his account of his experience at Auschwitz, he observed: "Because of the high degree of undernourishment which the prisoners suffered, it was natural that the desire for food was the major primitive instinct around which mental life centered."[28] Just as black slaves wrestled with the morality of stealing for, literally, their daily bread, Jews starving in the camps faced the same dilemma. Gisella Perl, another Auschwitz survivor, noted: "By stealing bread, shoes, water, you stole a life for yourself, even if it was at the expense of other lives." Perl concluded ruefully: "Only the strong, the cruel, the merciless survived."[29]

Black slaves and Jewish Holocaust victims also spoke of the lack of physical protection from cold weather. One black slave, Fanny Cannady, recalled the absence of shoes even in winter: "De chillum didn' have no shoes a-tall; dey went barefooted in de snow an' ice, same as 'twuz summertime."[30] In his Holocaust survivor memoir, Primo Levi echoed the outrage of the internees not having shoes to cover their feet. In the labor camps, shoes took on supreme importance; they were truly a matter of life and death, for "death begins with the shoes; for most of us, they show themselves to be instruments of torture, which after a few hours of marching cause painful sores which become fatally infected."[31]

Both slaves and camp internees wrote of other forms of deprivation and dehumanization. The auction of black males and females to be sold to plantations was an oft-mentioned dehumanizing aspect of slavery. James Martin described the experience of these slaves:

> The slaves are put in stalls like the pens they use for cattle. . . . At these slave auctions, the overseer yells, "Say, you bucks and wenches, get in your hole. Come out here." Then he makes 'em hop, he makes 'em trot, he makes 'em jump. "How much," he yells, "for this buck? A thousand? Eleven

hundred? Twelve hundred dollars?" Then, the bidders makes offers accordin' to size and build.[32]

For the concentration camp internees, liberation from the Allies brought a long-awaited end to the brutality and overt humiliations. But for the slaves, the constitutional amendments following emancipation in 1863 that were designed to give the newly freed blacks the same civil rights and protections afforded to other United States citizens did not end their experience of brutality and humiliation. Reconstruction failed in that the level of economic well-being and social integration never met a level that would allow one to speak of blacks as having equal rights, human respect, and fellow feeling from the larger white community. Polly Shine recalled: "The Reconstruction period has been hard on the Negro race, but we suffered it through, somehow. If we had another time like that to go through, I believes I would hang myself so as I would not suffer again."[33]

After the failure of Reconstruction (1865–77), and the emergence of the Ku Klux Klan and like-minded groups who were opposed to the incorporation of free blacks into American society, the oppression continued with the help of terror designed to frighten blacks into resuming a subservient role. Some survivors of slavery recalled the days in which the actions of the Ku Klux Klan brought fear to the emerging black community. Pierce Harper described it quite graphically:

After de colored people was considered free an' turned loose, de Klu Klux broke out. . . . De gov'ment built de colored people school houses, an' de Klu Klux went to work an' burn 'em down. Dey'd go to de jails an' take de colored men out, an' knocked deir brains out, an' break deir necks, an' throw 'em in de river.[34]

Brawley Gilmore remembered the terror of the Klan too: "We lived in a log house during the Ku Klux days. Dey would watch you just like a chicken rooster watching a worm. At night, we was skeered to have a light."[35]

The Particularity of Women's Suffering

Many black men, women, and children suffered from slavery. Many Jewish men, women, and children suffered and died during the Holocaust. But there was a particularity in women's suffering in both contexts that still has not received the amount of attention it deserves.[36] The reality is that black female slaves and Jewish female victims shared indignities reserved especially for oppressed women. Under the system of slavery, black women were subject to the whims and debased desires of white males. Linda Brent's story, chronicled in her slave narrative *Incidents in the Life of a Slave Girl*, vividly highlights the terror of the prospect of sexual assault, which was commonplace enough and always a possibility as young black girls matured during puberty:

> Everywhere the years bring to all enough of sin and sorrow; but in slavery the very dawn of life is darkened by these shadows. Even the little child, who is accustomed to wait on her mistress and her children, will learn, before she is twelve years old, why it is that her mistress hates such and such a one among the slaves. Perhaps the child's own mother is among those hated ones. She listens to violent outbreaks of jealous passion, and cannot help understanding what is the cause. She will become prematurely knowing in evil things.

Soon she will learn to tremble when she hears her master's footfall. She will be compelled to realize that she is no longer a child. If God has bestowed beauty upon her, it will prove her greatest curse.[37]

In Brent's own story, she shares her attempts to avoid the unwanted advances from her master and to seek, without success, some intervention from the master's wife, who knew what was happening.

Jacob Manson, a former slave, recalled the experience of one of the slave girls he knew: "One of de slave girls on a plantation near us went to her missus and tole her 'bout her marster forcing her to let him have somethin' to do wid her, and her missus tole her, 'Well, go on. You belong to him.' "[38] Young black women bore the children of their slave masters and sometimes suffered the trauma of having those children removed from them, particularly when the children strongly resembled the white children of the slave masters. Sometimes female slaves were involuntary breeders for masters who wanted to make more money. As former slave James Green observed about one particular master: "He breeds de niggers as quick as he can—like cattle—'cause dat means money for him."[39] The life of a black female slave of child-bearing age was one of unprotected vulnerability.

This particularized vulnerability of the female was an experience that Holocaust victims faced as well. Jewish women knew the humiliation of strip searches, lewd comments, and unwanted sexual advances from camp guards. Sonya Bernstein noted: "When the women were being searched for valuables and they didn't believe you and they searched down there . . . the screaming, it was terrible."[40] But perhaps worse than the humiliation from sexual assault was the terror that awaited women who were pregnant while in the camps. Olga Lengyel was a physician who served as an obstetrician in the camps. In her survivor memoir, she noted that "the word went around [in the camps] that it was extremely dangerous to be found pregnant."[41] She recounted the sad fate of those who successfully hid their pregnancies. Once these women delivered, *both* the mothers and their children were killed.

Not only did black female slaves and Jewish female camp internees suffer from this particularized vulnerability, but males closest to them suffered indirectly as well. What disturbed male slaves and male internment camp inmates most about the fate of the women they loved was the men's deep sense of helplessness in the face of the sexual exploitation of their women, because they were unable to offer any kind of protection.

The Brutality of Oppressors

Black slaves were sometimes subjected to acts of brutality by those who held them in bondage. Former slave Mary Reynolds noted with a gravity that bespoke a deep memory of slavery, despite having been emancipated decades before: "Slavery was the worst days that was ever seed in the world."[42] She described the experience as one in which "they was things past tellin'."[43] With a slave dialect and a matter-of-factness that did not obscure the graphic details, Reynolds described maltreatment at the hands of slaveholders:

> I seed them put the men and women in the stock with they hands screwed down through holes in the board and they feets [*sic*] tied together and they naked behinds to the world. . . . They cut the flesh 'most to the bones, and some they was, when they taken them out of stock and put them on the beds, they never got up again.[44]

Reynolds also noted that blacks were made to strip to the waist and were assaulted with a cat-o'-nine tails, which brought blisters to the skin. The blisters were then burst by the use of a wide strap of leather, which was fastened to a stick handle. She could see blood running down the back of "many" slaves, from the neck to the waist.[45]

Rachel Cruze, another slave, recalled that the overseers would pour salt-and-pepper water into the cuts to increase the slaves' suffering.[46] Former slave Thomas Cole expressed his protest against such violation, *as a human being*: "[He would] whip dem wid a cat-o'-nine tails till he bust de hide in lot of places 'cross deir backs. . . . Some people calls dem bullwhips, and dat is right for dem; *dey wasn't made ter whip people wid.*"[47] Even pregnant slaves were not exempt from either hard work or the beatings that were often part of the task of uncompensated labor.

The brutality of overseers and some slaveholders was matched, if not trumped, by the brutality of the death camps to resolve the "Jewish problem" in Europe. Aaron Hass notes what survivors of the death camps have described about their experiences at one particular camp, Flossenburg:

> "[The prisoners] were forced to line up in the bitter cold of December at Flossenburg, told to strip naked, and hosed down. More than one hundred at that *Appell* (roll call) froze to death."
>
> Hass notes that according to one survivor, "In the ghetto, there was a little child about four years old. And she was a very happy and friendly child. Even the Nazis liked to talk to her. One day she was walking alone and one of the Nazis asked her if she would like a candy. He said to her, 'Would

you close your eyes and open your mouth?' As she did so, he
shot her in the mouth."[48]

One can almost see the wisp of smoke from the revolver and the
spray of the child's blood and body tissue staining the sidewalk, as
the little girl dropped too quickly to register astonishment at the
unprovoked and unexpected fatal assault.

Fourteen-year-old Dawid Rubinowicz recorded in his diary
a similarly appalling act of the indiscriminate, senseless brutality
perpetrated by the gendarmes:

> Early this morning the gendarmes came. As they were driv-
> ing along the highway, they met a Jew who was going out of
> the town, and they immediately shot him for no reason, then
> they drove on and shot a Jewess, again for no reason. So two
> victims have perished for absolutely no reason.[49]

The horror of the brutality perpetrated against black slaves
and Jewish victims was exacerbated by the incredulity that one
human being could inflict that kind of pain and suffering upon
another. In such instances, the unwarranted brutality tended to
raise the question of the humanness of the *perpetrator* rather than
of the degraded victim.

The Agony of Nightmarish Transports

Long before they actually faced the dreaded transports to the
death camps, some Jews held a sense of dread about the prospects for their future. The Jews who remained in Germany after
1938 lived in fear and apprehension regarding their fate in a land
that had reduced them to alien status. Some of the most fearful
among them were only teenagers. For example, thirteen-year-old

Yitskhok Rudashevski recorded in his diary the sense of humiliation and heightened anxiety that had become commonplace within his community: "We are like animals surrounded by the hunter. The hunter on all sides: beneath us, above us, from the sides. Broken locks snap, doors creak, axes, saws. I feel the enemy under the boards on which I am standing."[50]

Later on Rudashevski recorded the sense of anguish that he and others like him grappled with: "To save one's own life at any price, even the price of our brothers who are leaving us. To save one's own life and not to attempt to defend it . . . the point of view of our dying passively like sheep, unconscious of our tragic fragmentation, our helplessness."[51]

Miriam Korber, another Jewish youth, also felt that anguish. But she expressed a sense of defiance all the same. Writing in her diary in the summer of 1942, she recorded the following:

> Today [July 16] is a sad day, very sad, just like at home, the day before the evacuation. . . . An evacuation now would be sure death. People's strength and the resources they brought from home are long gone. We are now tired, worn out, sapped of any energy; even if they left us alone, I think that many would not survive to see the end of the war. And as weak as we are, we are still a thorn in their eye, they try to destroy us. What an uneven battle. The German colossus and a handful of worn-out Jews.[52]

Later in 1942, sixteen-year-old Moshe Flinker noted in his diary:

> Last Friday afternoon . . . my father came in and told me that he had some bad news. He had heard that many Jews were dying in the East, and that a hundred thousand had already

been killed. When I heard this, my heart stood still and I was speechless with pain and shock. I had been fearing this for a long time, but I had hoped against hope that they really had taken the Jews for forced labor and that therefore they would have to feed, clothe, and house them enough to keep them alive. Now my last hopes have been dashed.[53]

A boy, whose identity was never established, testified to the turmoil he was experiencing, as recorded in his diary in July 1944:

I write these lines with anxiety and terrible grief—who knows what the next few days will bring us? Thousands have already been deported; tens of thousands more are going to be deported. In our present situation, when we have no strength left for walking on our feet, literally—deportation is a mortal danger for us—even if they don't kill us right away, we will die from the hardships along the way—and from starvation.[54]

Several months later, another youth, Eva Ginzova, wrote graphically of the sight of those on the transports:

My God, the things that are happening here now, it's difficult to describe. One afternoon [on April 20, 1945], I was at work when we saw a freight train go past. There were people sticking their heads out of the window. They looked awful! They were pale, completely yellow and green in the face, unshaven, emaciated, with sunken cheeks and shaven heads, dressed in prison clothes . . . and with a strange shine in their eyes . . . from hunger.[55]

Some time later, Ginzova saw "one transport after another" arrive with Hungarians, Frenchmen, Slovaks, Poles, and Czechs. Not only were there the beleaguered living but also the defeated dead: "And the number of dead among them! A whole pile in every car. Dressed in rags, barefoot or in broken clogs. It was such a terrible sight that hardly anyone had seen before. I wish I could express on paper all the things that are happening inside me."[56]

The depictions of the transports by survivors offer a gruesome picture of something that, in ordinary life, would have been unimaginable. Some of the most vivid portraits come from the pens of adult women. Lidia Rosenfeld Vago noted how she and others were herded into cattle cars, with more than eighty people to a car:

> No one had enough space to lie down or to sit on the floor with legs outstretched. Our rucksacks and shoulder bags served as seating cushions, and from time to time we stood up and sat down, to alleviate muscle pain. We were so cramped for space that it was quite a task to reach the toilet bucket in the middle of the car. The stench was unbearable. Those sitting close to the bucket held up sheets for some privacy, because, after all, we were civilized people.[57]

Olga Lengyel described the crowded, unsanitary, and completely uncomfortable conditions in the "cattle cars" this way: "Ninety-six men, women, and children in a space that would have accommodated only eight horses. Yet that was not the worst."[58] Indeed, that was *not* the worst: "The children cried; the sick groaned; the older people lamented; and even those who, like me, were in perfect health, began to pay attention to their own discomforts. . . . Soon the situation was intolerable."[59]

Men, women, and children struggled for a small space of their own. The cattle car—intended to accommodate only eight horses—turned into bedlam. To Lengyel, the cattle car, which had become an abattoir with the stench of the sick and the dead, became a "wooden gehenna."[60]

While the mass transport of the Jews took place over a period of several years during the Third Reich, the transport of black Africans from the so-called "dark" continent to the Americas occurred over a period of a couple of centuries. We do not have many accounts from the survivors of the Atlantic slave trade, but there are extant accounts of the transport of African captives from some of the slavers themselves and the physicians who treated the slaves on board. From these accounts, we know that the European slavers came on ships with such fanciful names as *Gift of God*, *Jesus*, *Liberty*, *Free Love*, and *Delight*, which belied the nature of their real mission.[61]

The extant depictions of the conditions of the slave ships of what came to be known as the Middle Passage reveal them to be every bit as horrific as the Jewish internee camps. Hapless Africans from the interior of the continent as well as the coastal regions were sometimes betrayed by rival tribespeople and nations. Some of the men, women, and youths were forced to march their way to the coast from the interior. Others were bound and taken on long rides on river canoes to locations where they would eventually board the waiting slave ships.[62] The slaves were guarded by fellow Africans and huddled in rows of shacks. Some were forced into castles and forts built by Europeans on the coasts. Others were settled in open clearings by the riversides.[63] The slavers warehoused their ill-gotten human booty in these grim and gory holding cells until a full cargo was ready, in order to maximize their profits.

Once on board the slave ships, the male slaves were manacled and shackled together, unable to position themselves comfortably as they lay pressed together, hardly able to breathe.[64] The chains and shackles cut into the flesh of the wrists and ankles as the slaves sought to position themselves. Under heavy guard by crew members poised at strategic locations throughout the ship to prevent escape and mutiny, the slaves were forced to live in the cargo area for weeks and months in conditions unfit even for animals.[65] The slavers herded as many as they could on one ship to maximize profits.[66] The cacophony of cries of lamentation, horror, and near despair, droning on in languages they could not understand, was enough to drive some into madness. Hundreds were felled by unfamiliar diseases as they lay in their own filth, and later their carcasses were tossed overboard like rotten meat.

The journey to the Americas could last up to three months. Between the time that a slave ship left a West African port until it docked in the Americas, the slave ships were vulnerable to drastic acts of resistance on the part of the newly captured. On occasion, the slaves were allowed on deck briefly for fresh air. Once on deck, some of them committed suicide, preferring to drown at sea rather than endure one more moment of the misery of the Middle Passage. Some starved themselves to death by successfully resisting attempts to force-feed them. Despite the precautions taken by the slavers, insurrections of the enslaved, as yet another form of resistance, were "not infrequent."[64] Although the number of revolts is unknown, most of the attempts failed. Because of the lack of records, it is impossible to know precisely how many slaves did not survive the transport to the Americas. However, historians estimate that between capture in Africa, the Middle

Passage, and initial exploitation in America, approximately five million African men, women, and children died as a result of the slave trade.[67] Eleven to twelve million African captives are said to have landed on American shores.[68] For those who did survive the journey, their agony continued as they reached ports up and down the Atlantic seacoasts.

On the slave ships, the captured Africans were herded like cattle into confined spaces in such a way that it was obvious that they were not viewed as human beings. The conditions were diabolically designed to make it clear that their well-being and comfort were of no concern to their captors. All of the cultural and social habits that accompany the human process of elimination and allow people to shade their personal grooming and hygiene rituals from prying eyes were completely ignored as the captives were housed together to await the further assault on their dignity and person. Their shame and loss of self-respect did not matter to their captors. As some of the "deported" died en route, their fellow travelers were forced to continue on with the putrid smell of the newly departed in their nostrils.

The Shame of One's Own Filth

Once in the camps, the Jewish internees experienced the utterly humiliating "assault of excrement."[69] One survivor recalled that at night the internees were forbidden to use the latrine. The only resource available to relieve themselves was the same brown bowls from which they had eaten their meager ration of soup.[70] Years later, Pelagia Lewinska recalled that the "assault of excrement" was part of the calculated effort to render the Jews devoid of their full humanity. Lewinska observed:

With all my heart I wanted to avoid passive acceptance, a prospect which filled me with fear. I did not understand the true purpose of a Nazi concentration camp. It was the latrines which finally pointed me toward the truth. The latrines consisted of a large ditch bisected by a narrow board which served as a perch. Even now I do not see the use of this tiny perch which, naturally, was always covered with filth. It was endlessly occupied on both sides. . . . Our backs practically touched and it was not rare for us to soil each other.[71]

With many in the camps suffering from typhus, dysentery, and other diarrhea-producing diseases, the struggle for privacy to meet basic needs for elimination and maintaining cleanliness, including access to soap and water and laundered clothes, contributed to the nightmarish experience of the camps. The human body, originally designed by the Divine to convey sublime beauty, was now the source of the stench and visible filth that assaulted the senses.

Terrence Des Pres explained the experience of the "excremental assault" in this way: "the stench of excrement mingled with the smoke of the crematoria and the rancid decay of flesh."[72] He and a number of survivors surmised that the "excremental assault" was part of the systematic task of attempting to rob the concentration camp internees of their visible dignity. In *The Survivor: An Anatomy of Life in the Death Camps*, Des Pres asked rhetorically: "How much self-esteem can one maintain, how readily can one respond with respect to the needs of another, if both stink, if both are caked with mud and feces?" For, in truth, "the prisoner was made to feel subhuman, to see his self-image only in the dirt and stink of his neighbor."[73]

Those first Africans who were stolen from their villages, sometimes with the help of Africans of other tribes, knew the degrading horrors of the "excremental assault" that were experienced by the Jews in the camps. As the African slave Olaudah Equiano recorded in his slave narrative in 1792:

The stench of the hold, while we were on the coast, was so intolerably loathsome, that it was dangerous to remain there for any time, and some of us had been permitted to stay on the deck for the fresh air; but now that the whole ship's cargo were confined together, it became absolutely pestilential. The closeness of the place, and the heat of the climate, added to the number in the ship, being so crowded that each had scarcely room to turn himself, almost suffocated us. This produced copious perspirations, so that the air soon became unfit for respiration, from a variety of loathsome smells, and brought on a sickness among the slaves, of which many died, thus falling victims to the improvident avarice, as I may call it, of their purchasers. This deplorable situation was again aggravated by the galling of the chains, now become insupportable; and the filth of necessary tubs, into which the children often fell, and were almost suffocated. The shrieks of the women and the groans of the dying rendered it a scene of horror almost inconceivable.[74]

Is it true then that those who had stopped washing, who had been unable to use the latrines, and who were assaulted by uncontrollable bouts of dysentery, had "the last remnants of [their] human dignity . . . burning out within [them]," as one camp internee was led to say?[75] It *would be* true if dignity is understood as "the projection of pretense and vainglory, or the ways power cloaks itself in pomp and ritual pride."[76] But in chapter 2, I will argue that human dignity is to be defined otherwise. I will deem it "indestructible," and I will demonstrate that "the last remnants of [their] dignity" did *not* "burn out within them." Rather, the inner protest that came from the souls of black slaves and Jewish internees soiled by their own waste in such "excremental assaults" bears witness to the indestructibility of their dignity.

Outrage at Degradation

Not only did black slaves and Jewish camp internees feel their degradation, but they chafed at the denial of their personhood. This experience of humiliation was the keenest sign of their inner protest against the kind of degradation that followed black slaves on plantations and the Jews in the camps. Thomas Cole observed that those who could not work—babies and very young children as well as the elderly and the infirm—were of little value because they could not produce: "Babies was to young ter work, and ole folks couldn't do much; besides, dey was liable to die at any time. Dey was mostly considered *worthless property*, after dey gits feeble."[77] Slaves were denied the privilege of exclusive service to God, as former slave Sarah Douglass observed: "We served our mistress and master, in slavery time, and not God."[78] The degradation started at the auction block. A former female slave remembers the peculiar indignity of female slaves at the auction block: "I 'members when they put me on the auction block. They pulled my dress down over my back to my waist, to show I ain't gashed and slashed up. That's to show you ain't a mean nigger."[79]

A fugitive slave named John Brown also recalled the indescribable experience of the auction block for slaves:

I do not think any pen could describe the scene that takes place at a negro auction. The companies, regularly "sized out," are forced to stand up, as the buyers come up to them, and to straighten themselves as stiffly as they can. When spoken to, they must reply quickly, with a smile on their lips, though agony is in their heart, and the tear trembling in their eye.[80]

Not surprisingly, the slaves dreamed of the possibility of owning their own bodies, recalls Edward Lycurgas, who met many runaway slaves who "one and all . . . had a good strong notion to see what it was like to own [your] and [body]."[81] Henry Bibb, a self-described *un*happy slave from Kentucky, recalls being "flogged up," rather than "brought up," on the plantation. He grew wistful in his slave narrative as he described the longing he himself felt to be free:

> Sometimes standing on the Ohio River bluff, looking over on a free State, and as far north as my eyes could see, I have eagerly gazed upon the blue sky of the free North, which at times constrained me to cry out from the depths of my soul, "Oh! Canada, sweet land of rest—Oh! When shall I get there?"[82]

But the dreams of Edward Lycurgas and the reverie of Henry Bibb, and of countless other slaves like them, remained unfulfilled and elusive. Mollie Dawson described the painful situation of the degraded slave:

> De slaves was about de same things as mules or cattle. Dey was bought and sold, and dey wasn't supposed ter be treated lack [*sic*] people anyway. We all knew dat we was only a race of people, as our master was, and dat we had a certain amount of rights, but we was jest property and had ter be loyal ter our

masers. It hurt us sometimes ter be treated de way some of us was treated, but we couldn't help ourselves and had ter do de best we could, which nearly all of us done.[83]

Charles Ball recalled the anguish he, too, felt in the system:

After we were all chained and handcuffed together, we sat down upon the ground; and here reflecting upon the sad reverse of fortune that had so suddenly overtaken me, and the dreadful suffering which awaited me, I became weary of life, and bitterly execrated the day I was born. . . . I longed to die, and escape from the hands of my tormentors; but even the wretched privilege of destroying myself was denied me, for I could not shake off my chains.[84]

With unmatched eloquence, William Wells Brown related in his slave narrative his agony over the impact of slavery upon the slave: "Slavery makes its victims lying and mean; for which vices it afterwards reproaches them, and uses them as argument to prove that they deserve no better fate."[85] But his love of liberty, which "burned in his bosom," led him to flee and sustained him in the struggle for the liberty of his people.[86] He wrote:

When I thought of slavery with its Democratic whips—its Republican chains—its evangelical blood-hounds, and its religious slave-holders—when I thought of all this paraphernalia of American Democracy and Religion behind me, and the prospect of liberty before me, I was encouraged to press forward, my heart was strengthened, and I forgot that I was tired or hungry.[87]

In a similar way, former slave Henry Bibb wrote about the indignity of slavery in his own slave narrative. He viewed himself as a "prisoner for life; I could possess nothing, nor acquire anything but what must belong to my keeper." He decried the theft of his liberty as follows: "No one can imagine my feelings in my reflecting moments, but he who has himself been a slave. Oh! I have often wept over my condition, while sauntering through the forest, to escape cruel punishment."[88] Kate Phoenix recalled of her life as a slave: "I knew I was unhappy, but I thought everythin' was like that. I didn't know there was happiness for nobody—me nor nobody."[89] Jack Maddox reported: "Our life was a misery. I hate the white man every time I think of us being no more than animals."[90] Belle Caruthers asserted: "I'm like the man that said, 'Give me freedom or give me death.'"[91] So much for the myth of the proverbial "happy" slave!

There was never any mythical notion of the "happy" concentration camp internee. The descriptions of their terror, as affirmed in newsreels of the liberation of the death camps, bear witness to the nightmarish reality of the "kingdoms of death." Before the transports, there were the large and small indignities that Jews experienced, which are reminiscent of some of the indignities that blacks suffered during the Jim Crow era. Bela Kornbluth recalled with righteous indignation not being permitted to walk on the same side of the street as a German: "We had to get off the sidewalk when a German approached. Can you believe that? . . . Why? Was I not a human being, too?"[92]

Bearing Witness: A Sign of Human Dignity

If the first sign of the indestructibleness of human dignity is the inner cry of protest, the second sign is the need of those who suffer unjustly to bear witness. Perhaps the greatest instance of commonality that binds the black experience of slavery and the Jewish experience of the Holocaust is the personal records that survivors of both left for posterity to tell the truth from the inside of what it was like to live through a heinous assault on their dignity as children of God. The telling of the story, the bearing witness of a crime against humanity, is a sure sign of the strength of human dignity—especially in such extreme situations. Again and again, Holocaust survivors who either record their experiences in narratives or share their testimony at lectures sponsored by the United States Holocaust Memorial Museum and other venues do so to ensure that the world will never forget what happened to European Jewry in the twentieth century. One Holocaust survivor, Olga Lengyel, claimed that she wrote her memoir, *Five Chimneys*, "to carry out the mandate given to me by the many fellow internees at Auschwitz who perished so horribly." She called *Five Chimneys* her "memorial" to them.[93]

In recounting the horrors of their experience, the desire has not been simply to shock but to paint a vivid picture that would evoke from the reader or hearer a *human* response to their violation. The telling and retelling of the experiences are not only a testimony to the tenacity of the human spirit but also an affirmation of the resilience of the glory bestowed upon the human— even the fallen human—by the most gracious God. It is in the need to bear witness, to record for posterity, to describe their pain and capture the profound depth of the assault, that we have a sign that, despite appearances, their dignity remained intact.

Most frightening to the survivors was not the details of the Nazi attempt to dehumanize them into extinction but the *silence*, the failure to speak up and bear witness to the truth of this assault not only against fellow human beings but against the God who made them. The prospect of silence was particularly horrifying to Sarah Berkowitz, author of *Where Are My Brothers?*

> This pitiful sound, which sometimes, goodness knows how, reaches into the remotest prison cell, is a concentrated expression of the last vestige of human dignity. It is a man's way of leaving a trace, of telling people how he lived and died. By his screams he asserts his right to live, sends a message to the outside world demanding help and calling for resistance. If nothing else is left, one must scream. Silence is the real crime against humanity.[94]

The prospect of silence haunted Elinor Lipper as well: "The silence of the Siberian graveyards, the deathly silence of those who have frozen, starved, or been beaten to death. This is an attempt to make that silence speak."[95] Bearing witness was so important to some in the camps that it was their main motivation to survive. Nadezhda Mandelstam observed as much when she said: "Whether inside or outside the camps, we had all lost our memories. But it later turned out that there were people who had made it their aim from the beginning not only to save themselves, but to survive as witness.[96] As Olga Lengyel rightly observed: "I knew that individual acts of revolt always brought mass reprisals at Auschwitz."[97] Survival was the perfect revolt because it enabled one to set the record straight for posterity.

Gisella Perl contended that one basic Nazi aim was to demoralize, humiliate, and ruin the Jews, not only physically but spiritually. In fact, "they did everything in their power to push us into the bottomless pit of degradation."[98] But it turns out that Aaron Hass was right when he asserted that "it is far easier to extinguish a man than to extinguish his memories."[99] Terrence Des Pres, author of *The Survivor: An Anatomy of Life in the Death Camps*, contends that for most survivors, to bear witness was the goal of their struggle.[100] They needed to be heard, to bear witness, to tell the world what they themselves had witnessed.[101] Hass also confirms the importance of survival in order to bear witness.[102]

Former slaves also felt the need to bear witness to their experience of human bondage. Many preface their stories with the observation that they have been led to offer testimony of their experience (or have been persuaded to do so) so that the larger public might know the truth regarding the nature of slavery and its terrible impact on the lives of those enslaved. The former slaves also wanted to offer their personal testimony in order to encourage others to persevere in the struggle for liberty. Henry Bibb probably said it best:

> The reader will remember that I make no pretension to literature; for I can truly say, that I have been educated in the school of adversity, whips, and chains. Experience and observation have been my principal teachers, with the exception of three weeks schooling which I have had the good fortune to receive since my escape from the "grave yard of the mind," or the dark prison of human bondage. . . . To be changed from a chattel to a human being, is no light manner. . . . And if I could reach the ears of every slave to-day, throughout the whole continent of America, I would teach the same lesson, I would sound it in the ears of every hereditary bondman: "break your chains and fly for freedom!"[103]

The need to tell others, the need to break the silence, seemed to the slaves and the camp internees like a sacred commitment they had to keep. The words and deeds of the oppressors were in danger of being misunderstood or even forgotten. Oral testimony and the written word were designed to ensure that those with eyes to see and ears to hear would know the truth and that, in the knowing, somehow the struggles of the survivors of human bondage and genocide would not be in vain.

A Common Humanity

What do these commonalities suggest about what it means to be human? As I reflect on the nature of the two distinct experiences—the black slaves and their struggle for freedom and the Jewish victims of Nazi Germany—I am struck to find more commonalities than one might initially imagine. The need to bear witness, the cry of the mother separated from her child, the humiliation from the stench of the excremental assault—all of these were human responses that arose from the experience of dehumanization. These shared commonalities between black slaves and Jewish internees demonstrate a depth of feeling and vulnerability. They testify to the capacity to suffer deeply, in the realm of the body, the emotions, and the spirit. We can imagine the horror and misery that we might have felt had we been in their places. This testifies to our common humanity.

The cries of protest of many of the black and Jewish victims were not always heard audibly. (In both contexts, revolts often brought severe retaliation against both the slaves and the camp internees.) Though the cry of their hearts may have been heard only by God, these children of God had no doubt that their maltreatment was a violation of their dignity that they could not bear in complete silence. By their testimony among those who had ears to hear, and by the written testimony of their narratives and memoirs, bearing witness was the single most important way the survivors had to affirm an inviolate dimension of human existence. It was a way of keeping the human spirit alive.

Perhaps "listening" to the testimonies does reveal a common humanity. What, then, does it mean to be human? The image of a black slave, with head bowed in shame and a sweaty body stooped by a load meant to be borne by a beast of burden, not a human being, does not evoke a sense of inherent value or inestimable worth. Nor does the naked, emaciated form of a European Jew, with hollow eyes that stare back vacantly at the lens of a camera, readily evince the biblical notion of humanity as the crown of creation. How incongruous it might seem to speak with credibility about human dignity in the context of black slavery and the Holocaust! And if, somehow, we can bring ourselves to speak of human dignity in such conditions, then surely it must be unthinkable to affirm the notion of dignity as being present in those who brought about unlivable conditions for the slave and for the concentration camp victims. The image of a malevolent overseer inflicting the pain of the lash on raw broken skin seems more akin to an ogre rather than to a compassionate soul who readily serves the weak. The image of a sadistic, brutal camp guard elicits the horror we would reserve for a monster, not for a fellow human being capable of love and affection. Nevertheless, though our initial impulse might lead us to do otherwise, our theological reflection must lead us to conclude that human dignity belongs to *both*: to the oppressed and the degraded and to the oppressor and the degrader.

Why is it important to uphold the dignity of both the enslaved and the degraded as well as the enslaver and the degrader? How can we keep both the oppressed and the oppressor in the same circle of humanity? Why is it even desirable to do so? What does it *mean* to be human, and what are the conditions of human dignity that make such a proposition possible? Why would it be necessary to affirm what may be for some a questionable article of faith? The answers to these questions lie not within the human creature but from the hand of God the creator. ■

Human Dignity: The Glory of Humanity

2

We are like animals surrounded by the hunter.

—YITSKHOK RUDASHEVSKI

They treated the colored folks like animals.

—MALINDA DISCUS

How is it that those who have been treated like animals are the appropriate context for defining human dignity? What can the dehumanized reveal to us about what it means to be human? Any notion of what it means to be human must be grounded in a context in which the human condition is revealed without pretense. What slave narratives and Holocaust survivor memoirs have described is the experience of men and women who have been brought to a low level at the hands of other men and women who were ultimately more degraded than they were. In the descriptions of experiences on slave plantations and death camps, we see human beings rendered naked (unmasked), defenseless, powerless, and extremely vulnerable. I maintain that this particular portrait of human beings may come closer to the truth about what it means to be human than any portrait of human beings in which they are supposedly at their "best." Robbed of pride and pretense, illusions of grandeur, and notions of complete independence, we are able to see human creatures as they really are, in all their vulnerability. An understanding of human dignity within the context of dehumanization calls attention to our interrelatedness, not simply as one species among many but also as the species whose distinctiveness is marked by some special connection to God.

The Human Being before God[1]

Over the centuries, Christian thinkers and philosophers have sought to define what it means to be human. In the 1930s, Christian ethicist and Lutheran pastor Reinhold Niebuhr published a two-volume study of the nature and destiny of human beings. In volume one of that work, *The Nature and Destiny of Man*, Niebuhr presents a historical analysis of the various ways that philosophers and theologians defined what it meant to be human throughout history. One great strength of Niebuhr's classic discussion of human nature is his recognition of the creaturely reality of human existence before God. By titling this section of his discussion as "the doctrine of man as creature," Niebuhr affirms at the outset the dependent, derivative character of the human being, a creature of God. Human beings have no independent existence. This dependent, derivative character is neither evil nor an inherent weakness that should evoke shame within the creature. As Niebuhr observed: "The whole biblical interpretation of life and history rests upon the assumption that the created world, the world of finite, dependent and contingent existence, is not evil by reason of its finiteness."[2]

In fact, the finitude, dependence, and insufficiency of humanity's earthly life "are facts which belong to God's plan of creation"[3] and should be accepted with reverence and deep humility. Our creaturely existence is a value that should be acknowledged, celebrated, and protected. The finitude that characterizes individual existence is a quality that describes the nature of our collective and national life as well. What precludes the fragmentary character of human life, whether individual or corporate, from being regarded as evil in biblical faith is the belief that each life and its meaning are connected to a divine plan that is in keeping with the will of God the creator. Thus, even though in both the Hebrew Bible and the New Testament we are reminded often of the brevity and fragility of life, the created world, and what dwells therein, is deemed "good." Its intrinsic goodness arises solely from the fact that God is the "author" of the good creation.

Niebuhr's insights here are invaluable for they anchor our discussion of what it means to be human in a theological framework that establishes a transcendent grounding for human existence. The human creature *belongs* to God, for without God the creature cannot exist. This existence is a gift of God, an instance of profound grace. Such a grounding, in which humans are understood as creatures *coram Deo* (before God), is the first line of defense against the denial of the intrinsic value and worth of every human being. This grounding also reinforces the notion of our interconnection not only to God but to one another and the rest of the created order. All that the human creature possesses is designed not only to serve the good of the individual but to contribute toward the well-being of the larger community as well. Moreover, this transcendent grounding indicates that life and death belong to God. No human being or group of human beings has legitimate "jurisdiction" over these matters. To usurp divine authority on these matters is to invite divine judgment.

There is more to what the biblical witness affirms about the nature of the human being before God that strongly concerns us as we reflect on the value of human life in an age in which that value is not always recognized. In the first account of creation in the book of Genesis, the biblical writer affirms the following notion of the human creature before God: "Then God said, 'And let us make humankind in our image, according to our likeness'" (1:26). At the command of God, at the speaking of the divine word, the human being was created in the "image" and the "likeness" of God. The Hebrew Bible and the New Testament maintain the importance of this initial affirmation about the human creature. Humanity did not create itself. God freely chose to create, and the human being is the culmination of God's creative efforts. And God pronounced this "very good." The human was blessed to be made in the image and likeness of God.

We do not know precisely in what way we image God. We do not know whether it is a physical trait, a particular faculty, a spiritual trait, or a capacity to do something, or whether the image of God is a constellation of characteristics. The Bible never defines what the *imago Dei*, the image of God, actually is.[4]

Although Christian thinkers have speculated as to what the image of God is, they have never denied the significance that the imprint of God bestows on the human being. As Niebuhr rightly notes, humanity in the biblical view of God is understood primarily from the standpoint of God rather than from any uniqueness of its faculties or its relation to the rest of nature.[5] Of significance to us is that whatever the dignity that accrues to human beings as a result of this imprint is, it is something that only God confers on us and that, because we are creatures of God, it is conferred on us all. This affirmation also implies that a certain sanctity is attached to us insofar as we come from the hands of God and that in some way we have been gifted with God's likeness. This indicates that our humanness as creatures of God, and the glory or sacred worth that derives from our humanness, is not something that we have earned or made ourselves but something that comes to us *from* God.

Human Dignity Defined

If, in some way, we image the creator God, this implies that some kind of dignity or glory surrounds who and what we are and that in some way we can (and must) recognize that dignity as something of value, something that warrants that each person be treated with respect and honor. The question of human dignity has received considerable attention in the contemporary social sciences, particularly as more attention has been given to the concept of universal human rights.[6] Despite the absence of consensus about the nature of human dignity, I believe it is not only possible but necessary to sketch an outline of the elements of this dignity for the purpose of our discussion. I have drawn key elements from the writings of Robert P. Kraynak, Timothy P. Jackson, Francis Fukuyama, and Raimond Gaita for my discussion of the concept of human dignity.[7]

This dignity reflects the stamp of the divine on us as creations made in the image of God. Like the image of God, this dignity (or glory) is something that only God confers on us all. This affirmation also implies that a certain sanctity is attached to us insofar as we come from the hand of God and that, in some way, we have been gifted with God's likeness. This indicates that our humanness as creatures of God and the glory or sacred worth that derives from our humanness are not something that we have earned or made ourselves. This dignity is never to be confused with being "dignified." It is a decidedly graced aspect of who we are in our creatureliness. As a gift, it is not something we can earn. It is not connected with what we do or fail to do. It is not related to our conduct. Thus, even those who commit heinous crimes are entitled to the respect that comes by virtue of being human (again, this emphasizes the *grace* of our humanness). Human dignity is given to *all* humans, regardless of abilities, capabilities, or disabilities, physical or mental.[8] This dignity is not mitigated by our economic, social, or political status or our gender. This dignity is granted to us from the beginning of life and follows us to the grave.

Human dignity is indestructible. Because it is God's gift to us, it cannot be taken away from us by others. This dignity or glory is also indestructible because it reflects the image of God in us, which is also indestructible. Of course, human dignity or glory can be obscured, assaulted, and hidden—for we see this as we read about the experiences of Jewish men, women, and children of the Holocaust. We can also see much degradation as we read about the experiences of black men, women, and children who endured the indignities of slavery and Jim Crow. There is no doubt that a systematic and repeated assault on our dignity can distort the human spirit and deform the personality. However, regardless of our circumstances—in spite of the fact that it may be difficult at times to see ourselves or others as humans worthy of respect once we or they have been humiliated, persecuted, and scorned—our dignity remains because this human glory comes from God alone. I would argue that when attempts are made to assault that dignity, the cry of protest, whether vocal or muted, is indeed a staunch testimony to the ultimate indestructibility of this dignity. This indignant cry of protest from deep within the soul is a rebuke and a judgment against the attempted violation that reverberates in the heavens.

There is a social dimension to this dignity. This social dimension is marked by the human need to have our person-hood acknowledged or affirmed. To have a sense of well-being, we must respect the dignity of others as we would want our own dignity respected. This need for reciprocity or mutuality of acknowledgement is so powerful that when it is denied, it increases our suffering. As we saw in chapter 1, the slave narratives and the Holocaust survivor memoirs both indicate that what made the victims' hardships more difficult to bear was that they were not treated as human beings. Their dignity was not acknowledged. This absence of regard for their humanity in the midst of maltreatment and deprivations multiplied their suffering.

This aspect of the social dimension of human dignity is best expressed by the moral philosopher Raimond Gaita. Gaita eloquently articulates the need for such acknowledgment of one's dignity in this way: "Treat me as a human being, fully as your equal, without condescension." The deliberate, systematic denial of that need for equality of respect exacerbates the experience of any material deprivations one might be forced to suffer. As Gaita writes: "Those who are the victims of injustice suffer not merely certain determinate forms of natural harm—physical or psychological damage, for example—but also the *injustice of their infliction*, which is a distinct and irreducible source of torment to them."[9] This social dimension of dignity means that our humanness is tied to that of every other human being. It means that our humanity is completed in the presence of others who also know our value and worth. When we lose sight of our value and worth or that of others, it becomes ever so easy to treat others as less than human.

The shame we feel for the violation *of others* is the flip side of the social dimension of human dignity. We are quite capable of experiencing repugnance, a sense of horror, and a heaviness of heart in response to the dehumanization of others. Their protest can reverberate in our own hearts. In turn, in our own souls, *we* can protest the betrayal of that which is sacred in others. That instinctual recoiling from the violent offense against the dignity of a fellow human being testifies to the reality of the presence of the *imago Dei* in all of us and the kinship it brings. Every attempt to deny or obscure it in ourselves and others will leave us feeling diminished if our hearts have not been hardened.

It should be clear from this discussion that this concept of human dignity has nothing to do with the attempts human beings may make to elevate themselves in the eyes of fellow human beings, usually at the expense of others. It is closer to the understanding of Terrence Des Pres, who writes that dignity is "an inward resistance to determination by external forces; a sense of innocence and worth, something to be inviolate, autonomous and untouchable, and which is most vigorous when most threatened—this is a constituent of humanness, one of the irreducible elements of selfhood."[10]

Ultimately, despite attempts to violate it, human dignity—as a reflection of the glory of the *imago Dei*—cannot be touched. It is that particular dimension of us that essentially defines us as human beings. The indestructibleness of that dignity becomes most clear when attempts are made to degrade or dehumanize a human being.

The Human Face and Dignity

It may well be difficult for us to get a full sense of the concept of human dignity as representing the glory of the image of God in us in the abstract. We may ask whether there is a way we might have a visual representation of this dignity. I would like to suggest that the human face is that concrete, visual representation. Here, I draw inspiration from the work of the late philosopher Emmanuel Levinas. The ethical demand to be viewed, acknowledged, and treated as a full human being can be seen in Levinas's concept of "the face."

Levinas himself was a Jewish Lithuanian survivor of a German prisoner-of-war camp. The Holocaust and his experience of it were the backdrop for his work as a philosopher in France. The theme of his philosophy is that the philosophical task begins with ethics and that ethics begins in the face of the Other.[11] Levinas saw himself as attempting a "phenomenology" of sociality, in which he took as his point of departure the face of the Other, which, before anything else, commands that we not remain indifferent to the death of the Other.[12] It is in the face that we meet the commandment "Thou shalt not kill."[13] "The face" is the best known and the most mysterious concept in Levinas's thought.[14] It has great possibilities as a foundation for ethics.

But interpreters of Levinas are constantly warned not to confuse the Levinassian face with anything we might *see*. We are urged not to interpret his concept of the face as a physical, observable part of a human body. For Levinas, the face is, before all else, the channel through which otherness presents itself to us, and as such it lies outside and beyond what can be seen or experienced.[15] Levinas's discussion of the face has an elusive quality that is problematic. Although I see great possibilities in his articulation of the concept of face, I find some aspects of his concept wanting. So, at the great risk of rendering Levinas's concept of the face more concrete and much less elusive than he would ever have chosen it to be, I contend that the physicality of the face is crucial for a conception of human dignity that is concrete. Sustained reflection on the photographs of slaves and ex-slaves and of concentration camp internees compels us to employ language that attests to the *physicality* of the human experience. In particular, the faces of the dehumanized cry out for a discussion of human dignity that is concrete and physically palpable.

I also contend that the face functions as a synecdoche—that is, the face stands not only for the actual face but for the entire body as well. The visual testimony of the photographs of slave and camp internee witnesses indicate in poignant, graphic detail that the attempt to violate the glory of the human made in the image of God is often vividly reflected in the body. Whether it is the sting of the lash, the searing burn of a bullet, the sharp pain from a machete, or the denial of nourishment, it is often in the realm of the body that we are first abused. Thus, the human beings we encounter in our daily walk confront us in the form of the face, with a visible, concrete manifestation of their value and worth in the eyes of God. This worth suggests a sacredness that we must not breach. The sacredness that we can see in the face of another says not only, as Emmanuel Levinas asserts, "Thou Shalt not Kill," but also "You are connected to me."

Fortunately, it is not the comeliness of the human face that garners our respect and honor. So one can have a face that only a mother could love, but it is still a face that all are bound to respect. The body we are given might never be aesthetically pleasing to us—particularly if we are women. Nevertheless, it is through the face—through the body—that our dignity as creatures of God shines forth and calls us to respond with respect, to treat each one as having inestimable value.

Insofar as each one of us bears the mark of God, this mark connects us theologically to each and every person. This connection is the link that makes it incumbent on us to be keepers of one other. Thus, what happens to you concerns me, and, likewise, what happens to me concerns you. This connection transcends familial ties, racial and ethnic categories, national allegiances, and whatever distinctions we would choose to make that allow us to divide the world between "us" and "them." The affirmations that we are creatures who live *coram Deo* and are created in the image of God, and the implications that arise from these affirmations, are two theological principles central to reflection on what it means to be human in a world in which forms of slavery still exist, a world where it appears easy to perpetrate unspeakable acts of brutality against even those we do like and to annihilate those who do not conform to our standards and mores.

Even in contemporary texts, many theologians have written about what it means to be human without speaking of the notion of human dignity. However, in our time, we *must* speak of it. Ironically, we cannot afford to think about human dignity or glory in the context of human achievement, where, through our gifts and graces, we soar in the heights of human potential. Instead, we must ponder the notion of dignity in the dirty hovels of human existence. For me, black slavery and the Jewish Holocaust provide the surprising but perfect contexts in which to look at what it means to be human, because it is in the depths of degradation that we are driven to ponder the true nature of humanity.

In these contexts, dignity itself does not allow our gaze to pass over people who suffer unjustly, without great cost not only to our brothers and sisters but also to ourselves. In fact, it is such contexts that heighten the question of what it means to be human because they force us to ask whether there is indeed some point in our own existence in which we could lose our humanness at our own hands or at the hands of others. If we could lose our humanity, if it could be taken away from us, then we would live always teetering at the abyss that leads to moral chaos. If we could lose our dignity, then we would be at the mercy of others.

Yet, even as we dare to speak boldly about the human glory that comes from being made in the image of God, a glory that indeed confronts us, we must also, at the same time, speak truthfully about the threats to that dignity through the actions of individuals, groups, communities, and nations. Those actions I call the sin of defacement.

The Sin of Defacement

A discussion of the word *defacement* can help elucidate the relationship of sin to human dignity. The sin of defacement is the assault on the dignity of another. To deface others is to deny them the respect and honor due to them by virtue of their full humanity.

It is to fail to see their sacredness. It is to denigrate the temple of the Holy Spirit. It is to dismiss such persons as having no value or worth. It is to say that they do not matter, that they have no place in God's world. It is an erasure of their presence and a challenge to their right to exist. Defacement can be a violent expression of sin. History has shown that we ignore or deny the significance of the face, the body, the temple of the Holy Spirit, at our own peril.

The range of acts that can be classified as defacement extends from the humiliating snub of being treated as invisible by the clerk in a store to genocide. Individually or personally, we commit defacement when we render people invisible or inconsequential. It can happen when we walk past people in the hall on a daily basis without ever bothering to acknowledge their existence. It happens when we hurry past the panhandler who demands a dollar. The sin of defacement can be corporate or communal, when our communities engage in activities that exclude other racial and ethnic groups from the advantages of a decent life by denying them access to the benefits of good neighborhoods, decent schools, and well-paying jobs. The sin of defacement can become embedded into legislation and social policies that make it legal and the natural order of things to keep minorities from the opportunities needed to participate effectively in national life.[16] The sin of defacement is probably most visible when one group in a society decides that another group is not fit to live.

The sin of defacement in its most violent forms seems omnipresent in our day. The practice of slavery, which African Americans endured until its end after a bloody civil war in the nineteenth century, has continued in another guise through the twentieth century and into the twenty-first. This new form of slavery is called debt bondage, and it afflicts children, women, and men—particularly in Asia, parts of Africa, and places in Latin America.[17] In the twentieth century, we saw four or five genocides, depending on where members of the international community settle as they haggle over the definition of the "G-word." Although after the Holocaust it was thought that a civilized world would never let genocide happen again, two of the *acknowledged* genocides have occurred *after* the Holocaust. And the relentless killing goes on. The act of identifying other people as the enemy is the first step toward the process of deathly dehumanization. The enemy is a monster—a hated, vile *thing* that must be subdued, dominated, tortured, and ultimately destroyed.

In the context of an understanding of human dignity in theological terms, defacement is a denial of the goodness of God's handiwork. It renders us judges over who is allowed to live and who must die. When truly understood, a theological conception of human dignity forces us to renounce all forms of defacement. It calls us to acknowledge and affirm a divine basis for the common bond between us. It gives us a religious basis for cultivating a culture of concern for each other, particularly the ones who are lodged precariously along the margins. It gives us a basis for challenging the nature of our economic, social, and political systems, which hinder our life together. This theological conception of human dignity, rightly understood, leaves us no choice but to recognize that human dignity is also a social and political reality.

As important as it is in a day and time in which some lives are treated as dispensable, we must speak about the dignity that accompanies the human person, especially as we clamor for the protection of human rights. Yet, even as we dare to speak boldly about the human glory that comes from being made in the image of God, we must also, at the same time and with the same importance, speak truthfully about the defacement that works to obscure and assault the dignity of others. These two descriptors of the human condition—dignity and defacement—must be held in tension as we articulate further the social and political nature of the sin of defacement. In the next three chapters, I will address the concept of the sin of defacement in terms of its communal and sociopolitical manifestations in the context of black slavery and the Jewish Holocaust. ▦

Anti-Semitism and Black Antipathy: Early Patterns of Dehumanization

3

We served our mistress and master, in slavery time, and not God.

—Sarah Douglas

I sank to my knees with the words that preside over human life: "And God made man after His likeness." That passage spent a difficult morning with me.

—Etty Hillesum

At first glance, anti-Semitism and white supremacy seem like disparate phenomena because they plagued distinct populations and because their respective historical trajectories have been somewhat different. Nevertheless, a comparison and contrast are justified because they share common features that establish the nature of defacement as a communal or corporate expression of sin. A comparison between these two phenomena is also justified because both forms of prejudice share a historical moment in which the negative, hostile sentiments toward their respective populations evolved into ideologies at the dawn of modernity. Later, I will demonstrate that anti-Semitism and white supremacy are two forms of racism with a common theological foundation. But, in this current chapter, we will look briefly at the emergence of anti-Semitism and white supremacy in their respective historical beginnings.

Anti-Semitism before the Enlightenment

Anti-Judaism has had a long history. Studies of this phenomenon often begin with an examination of anti-Judaism in the Roman Empire, although this prejudice was present even in the ancient world. Ancient anti-Jewish writings reveal hostility toward Jews because of Judaism's monotheism, which non-Jewish writers perceived as threatening to the social order. However, from the first century onward, anti-Judaism acquired a transcendent, more universal quality, integrally connected with religious teachings in a way that had not been present before.[1] Originally, the church's relationship to Israel was envisioned as one of ongoing fellowship between the Jewish and the Gentile branches of Christianity.[2] However, gradually, as tensions prevailed between Jewish and Gentile Christians, the latter branch took the view that the difference between Jews and Gentiles had been erased. Therefore, the continuation of Jewish rituals and practices by Jewish Christians was forbidden. With the outlawing of those practices in the Christian community, along with the notion that the corporeal body of Israel was deemed superfluous, supersessionism became a feature of Christian theology and praxis.

Supersessionism, which has implicit strains in some of the New Testament writings, is the traditional Christian view that held that the coming of Christ eliminated the theological significance of the distinction between Jew and Gentile.[3] It encompasses the belief that the church has replaced Israel as the bearer of God's election.[4] The doctrine of the church's supersession of Israel as the people of God "has been a leitmotif of Christian theology from patristic times to this day."[5] Supersessionism has served as the grounds for Christian anti-Semitism since the breach between Jewish and Gentile Christians became final.

With respect to the role of Christianity in fostering and perpetuating anti-Judaism, historians have determined that preaching, pastoral letters, theological writings, decrees of church officials, oral tradition, and even passages in the New Testament itself helped to create the intellectual, emotional, and religious justifications for the anti-Semitism that would taint the Christian church throughout Western history. The charge that Jews were Christ-killers and collectively responsible for the crucifixion of Jesus and the charge that the scattering of the Jews, which coincided with the Roman siege of Jerusalem in 70 CE, was a punishment for the crime of deicide, were the two critical, distinctively Christian contributions to the development and support of anti-Semitism.[6]

In the period of early Christianity, anti-Semitism affected the Jews in various ways. They were subject to discriminatory taxation and were prohibited from engaging in forms of religious practice. They were also expelled from the larger society and forced into ghettoes that isolated them from others. The Jews were also accused of being dishonest, lazy, and prone to sexual perversions and license, which undoubtedly made them easy targets for physical abuse and general harassment.[7] These forms of persecution came with the blessings of church officials.

The medieval period, which included such events as the Crusades, the devastating bubonic plagues, the sixteenth-century Reformation, and the Spanish Inquisition, saw the alteration of the character of the old religious prejudices that had marked the anti-Semitism of the early church. The writings of such esteemed Christian thinkers as Thomas Aquinas, who advocated the permanent servitude of the Jews,[8] and Martin Luther, whose vicious anti-Jewish tirades in his later writings gave more ammunition to the charge of Christianity's shameful contribution to the sordid events of twentieth-century Europe, demonstrate the way in which anti-Semitism permeated the medieval church.[9]

Two developments in the canon of charges against the Jews emerged during this period: (1) the reintroduction of the libelous charge that Jews were guilty of ritual murder in their religious practices and (2) the newer charge that the Jews perpetrated such desecrations of the host as stabbing the host (which signified the re-crucifixion of Jesus); tearing, spitting, or walking on the host (to show contempt for the Savior); burning the host; mixing it with excrement; and using it to make poison.[10] Unfortunately, both of these libels were taken seriously and led to much suffering for Jews.[11] Jews in the Middle Ages were subject to older forms of persecution, but there was also a new, insidious twist to how they were perceived by the larger population. During the medieval period, with the tragedy of the Black Plague, the long-standing myth of Jews as master conspirators emerged. The Jews were blamed for the devastation wrought by the bubonic plague, which was perceived as a plot to exterminate Christians. From the medieval period on, it became easier to scapegoat Jews for whatever misfortunes struck the larger society.[12] By the time of the Inquisition, even conversion to Christianity would not be sufficient to enable them to escape persecution.

Through the centuries, the pariah factor served to dehumanize Jewish men, women, and children by either investing them with tremendous power to affect adversely the lives of others or ascribing to them negative and obnoxious traits that denied them the full range of human conduct, emotion, and experience. Because Jews were viewed as "deliberate unbelievers," and undoubtedly were doubly disparaged for their infidelity to God, they were stereotyped as users, bribers, secret killers, sorcerers, magicians, and oppressors of the poor.[13] As such, it became not only easier but even *praiseworthy* to see them as less than human.

The Age of Reason (1648–1789), with its sometimes strident celebration of the emancipation of humanity from the tyranny of religious and state authority, led to a shift in the character of anti-Semitism from religious anti-Judaism to a secular brand that was based, ironically, on the caricatures and stereotypes that actually arose from religious anti-Judaism. The Enlightenment—which ushered in expansion of political power, economic wealth, technological innovations, advances in scientific inquiry, and an aversion to religious and secular authority—saw the rise of such figures as Voltaire, Thomas Hobbes, Rene Descartes, Immanuel Kant, and Jean Jacques Rousseau, among others, who would champion new ways of viewing humankind, emphasize self-determinism (for some), and celebrate liberation from the burdensome shackles that had theretofore prohibited the freedom of conscience of men. In territories where secularism, democratic revolutions, scientific developments, and the attendant accoutrements of modernism were welcomed, outright slaughter of the Jews declined. However, the initial sense of optimism that erupted as a result of these new developments was shattered in the nineteenth century, when the primary foundation for anti-Semitism shifted from the Christian doctrine of supersessionism to secular, pseudoscientific racial theories.

Although religious anti-Judaism helped sustain the contempt for the Jews that would allow persecution and even annihilation as a possibility, it must be said that with the emergence of modernity, anti-Semitism took on a distinctively different tone and the doctrine of supersessionism was replaced by a racial ideology that lead to wholesale slaughter of the Jews. Under the pretext of jettisoning authority over the conscience of men, be it religious or secular, the Enlightenment continued to carry forth ideas about the Jews that came from religious prejudice. However, without the evangelistic concerns that sustained religious anti-Semitism, this prejudice morphed into a form of anti-Judaism as virulent as, if not more so than, the religious form of anti-Judaism. This latter form was consistent with idolatry in the same way that white supremacy was, even though the Jews were never a "race" in the biological sense of the nineteenth-century understanding of the term. Whether Jews were persecuted because of their religious affiliation or because of their cultural identity, the dignity and worth of Jews were thrown into question by those who objected to their presence in society *because they were Jews.*

Black Antipathy and Slavery before the Enlightenment

The shift from black antipathy to white racism—or, more precisely, to white supremacy—in the United States occurred gradually, over a period of two centuries, despite the fact that the nation was founded on the principle of liberty and was influenced early on by an egalitarianism that had been shaped by revival movements within Protestantism. The institution of slavery was intricately tied to growing anti-black sentiment. As slavery prospered, particularly in the southern portion of the United States, blacks were eventually viewed as uniquely suited for enslavement. Racial prejudice and theories of race were not unknown before colonial expansion to the Americas, but the significance of them for the progression from garden-variety ethnocentrism to full-fledged white supremacy took nearly two centuries.[14] The contact of English colonists first with Native Americans and soon afterward with Africans in the New World led to the formation of institutions and relationships that would later be used to justify appeals to race for the extermination of Native Americans and the enslavement of blacks.[15]

When slavery first reached the British colonies of North America, there had been only a minimum of racial theory,[16] although there probably was a caste barrier between whites and blacks sometime before the institution of legalized slavery.[17] The link between black antipathy and the inauguration of the Atlantic slave trade occurred as a result of the monopolization of blacks for slavery. At the time the slave trade from Africa to the Americas started, human bondage had been an age-old phenomenon. The practice of slavery can be traced to the ancient world, and this common practice was noted in both the Hebrew Bible and the New Testament. However, slavery in the past had generally been a by-product of war or a means of debt relief and was usually prescribed for only a certain period of time. Previously, slavery did not preclude social mobility nor was it hereditary—that is, passed down from generation to generation. It did not involve laws designed expressly for the purpose of dehumanizing the enslaved.

The European enslavement of Africans to labor without remuneration in the New World represented a marked change in the scope and character of slavery. When the use of indigenous people of the Western Hemisphere, poor white prisoners and indentured servants of Europe, and slave workers in the Americas proved unsuccessful, Africans were chosen as servants in this new system of slavery. Africans were far from home, had no natural allies to fight for them, and had no means of putting political pressure on those who could put an end to the supply of slaves. Furthermore, because they were non-Christians, nonwhite, and viewed as foreigners by the Europeans, they became the "elect"—the crowned inheritors of a system of exploitation that linked economic prosperity with ethnocentric antipathy. These elect, judged to be uniquely suited for slavery, provided the back-breaking labor that would help to make the United States a prosperous nation.[18]

Once the Atlantic slave trade proved profitable in the southern portion of the United States, repressive laws were enacted to protect the slaveholders rather than the slaves. The character of this ancient practice of forced labor became a tool to deprive systematically men, women, and children of African descent of the means to live out their lives in freedom of movement and equal opportunity to fulfill their God-given potential to lead productive, satisfying lives. These laws, commonly referred to as Black Codes, regulated every aspect of the slaves' existence. Infractions of these codes brought the threat of a lash and other brutal forms of retaliation.

At the heart of the codes was the notion that slaves were not persons but property. In order to safeguard that "property," these laws had to ensure both the domination of the slave by the master and the protection of the master from any insubordination of the slave. The slaves did not have political or civil rights, nor did they have any legal standing in the courts. They could not be legally married. They could not defend themselves from whites; they could be put to death if they killed a white person, even in self-defense. Slaves could neither own livestock nor buy or sell goods, unless acting on behalf of the master. They were prohibited from learning to read or write. They could not assemble for worship or otherwise congregate in groups without supervision by whites. Each time a revolt of the "happy" slaves occurred, harsher laws were passed to control them. They were denied the right to self-determination and even the exclusive right to their own bodies. Their lives were neither God's nor their own.[19]

Although white supremacy was not the initial motivation for the inauguration of the Atlantic slave trade during the late seventeenth century, *black* slavery would not have become so deeply an entrenched institution without the growing strength of white supremacy. While other populations, such as indigenous people in the Americas, were also victims of slavery, by the eighteenth century blacks were viewed as innately suited for enslavement and even free blacks were treated with contempt and hostility *because they were black*. With the emergence of modernity, white supremacy assumed a strength and power that would extend far beyond the Civil War and the legal emancipation of blacks from slavery. White supremacy led to the birth of Jim Crow—legalized segregation of blacks and whites in the South (and de facto segregation in many parts of the North)—and these laws would not be successfully challenged until the modern civil rights movement, which began in the mid-1950s.

Patterns of Dehumanization

As you can see from this brief survey of anti-Semitism and black antipathy connected with slavery, these patterns of dehumanization were present in some form in the ancient world. The sin of deface-ment is reflected in both phenomena by several common features. First, both anti-Semitism and black antipathy were characterized by their identification of "in-groups" and "out-groups" within the society that practiced them. In Europe and other places, non-Jews represented the in-group; Jews, the out-group. In Europe, and later in its colonies, those of African descent were identified as the out-group. Second, the out-group became victims of the pariah factor, whereby the out-group had been invested with a variety of negative traits, embellished through unfair caricatures, which led the more powerful in-group to isolate them from the rest of the population. In the case of Jews, they were characterized as greedy, mercenary, deceitful, and deviously shrewd. With regard to peoples of African descent, they were invariably characterized as childish, shiftless, lazy, and licentious.

Third, enforced segregation from the body politic led to the suffering that results from ostracizing. The movements of Jews and blacks within society were restricted. They were denied basic liberties. They were effectively "marked" so as to ensure that they did not easily mingle with members of the in-group. (Of course, with regard to blacks, this "marking" was effortless due to their skin color and other physical features.) Fifth, in order to keep the pariah factor alive, the out-group was constantly beleaguered by characterizations that always placed them in a negative light. They were invested with relentlessly unflattering character traits, effectively robbing them of the full range of human traits that the rest of the human family shares. This constituted a denial of the full humanness of members of the out-group.

The suffering engendered by the communal pressure of the larger society led to physical, mental, and spiritual suffering. No matter what they did or refrained from doing, they were unable to escape their designation as a member of the out-group. Finally, participation in sustaining the pariah factor of the out-group was one of the surest ways that an in-group member could elevate his or her status within the in-group and be viewed as one who upholds the "purity" of the caste system, for this "purity" is seen as a positive good. (Likewise, one of the quickest ways to incur the wrath of the in-group is to engage in conduct that suggests sympathy toward members of the out-group. The taunts of "Jew lover" and "nigger lover" have often dampened the instincts responsible for fellow feeling or courage to opt for fellowship between members of the in-group and the out-group.)

These patterns of dehumanization are concrete examples of communal defacement. In anti-Semitism, the dignity of the Jew was neither respected nor honored. In early black antipathy, the sacredness of their humanity before God was neither seen nor acknowledged. The Jew and the black were dismissed as persons without value or worth. In fact, in some instances, the respective in-group harbored a belief that the Jew and the black had no rightful place in God's world. As a result of this defacement, in the case of Jews the stage was being set for an erasure of their presence in the continent of Europe. In the case of blacks, their fate was centuries of servitude and debasement.

As can be seen from this brief survey, racial anti-Semitism and white racism were already destructive and morally problematic. However, with intellectual developments in modernity, these forms of prejudice hardened into even more life-denying forms of defacement during the nineteenth and twentieth centuries. Although anti-Semitism and white supremacy took different paths in the lives of two different populations, the forms of prejudice that spawned them share a significant theological underpinning that binds them together in terms of what it does and does not mean to be human. In the next chapter, we will examine the constellation of factors whose genesis in the Enlightenment period established that anti-Semitism and white supremacy share a common theological cause. ■

Racism and Anti-Semitism in Modernity

4

Dey was mostly considered worthless property, after dey gits feeble.

—Thomas Cole

We were really no longer human beings . . . but putrefying corpses on two legs.

—Reska Weiss

The point has been made that black antipathy and anti-Semitism were present in the ancient world. However, they emerged with a new cast at the threshold of modernity. On the one hand, confidence in human progress and faith in science, fed by black antipathy, were used to *justify* economic and political interests that supported the institution of slavery and sustained the degradation of black people well into the twentieth century. Confidence in the human capacity to conquer new horizons in this new emancipation from religious and state authority, and faith in the emerging new social sciences, became the intellectual scaffolding for supporting the economic and political interests of slaveholders.

As the black population continued to grow and fears increased about the possibility of blacks and whites living together in American society, antipathy toward blacks intensified. These concerns led whites to use the work of social scientists regarding the alleged innate inferiority of blacks to sustain not only the institution of slavery but also the continued degradation of African Americans long after slavery ended. Anti-black sentiment was a reality both in the North, which had far fewer blacks and which profited less directly from slavery, and in the South, where the institution was the region's main source of economic welfare. But with sectional tensions and the South's increasing intransigence over the question of slavery, pseudo-scientific theories that upheld notions of black inferiority were used to shore up support for the sanctity of the "peculiar" institution against increasing threats to it from abolitionists.

On the other hand, confidence in human progress and faith in science were used to *fortify* long-standing Jewish antipathy, which sanctioned the pervasive scapegoating of the Jews in the context of economic, social, and political unrest in the twentieth century. Confidence in the human capacity to conquer new horizons in this new emancipation from religious and state authority, and faith in the emerging new social sciences, became the intellectual scaffolding for heightening long-standing Jewish antipathy. This scapegoating seemed to be the answer to the economic, social, and political unrest and resultant instability in Germany. It also served as a rallying point for Germans as they sought to overcome the stigma and humiliation of defeat in World War I. Although centuries-old Christian anti-Semitism remained a factor in the German church's capitulation to National Socialism, a secular dimension of this ancient prejudice ratcheted up the discrimination against the Jews in such a way to make it seem not only justifiable but *necessary* to carry out the implications of this prejudice to its logical conclusion: extermination of European Jewry.

Several elements of the Enlightenment project greatly contributed to the shift in tone in black and Jewish antipathies in the nineteenth and twentieth centuries. These elements reshaped old prejudices into more virulent forms. They catapulted human defacement beyond the individual and corporate levels into fully developed structural and systemic embeddedness, which marginalized black slaves and Jews in their respective environments in ways that would lead to psychic and even physical destruction. By the nineteenth and twentieth centuries, the modernity project would be revealed, with cruel irony, as the very antithesis of "enlightenment" and as one of the biggest purveyors of human defacement.

The Age of Reason

The Enlightenment, also known as the Age of Reason (1648–1789), emerged as a legacy of the Protestant Reformation and the resulting wars, bloodshed, and conflict arising out of the interplay of religion and politics over many centuries. The Peace of Westphalia (1648) marked a formal end to the Thirty Years' War. This series of religious and political wars left a bitter taste that led intellectuals to believe that emancipation from dogmatic religious and political authorities would afford much greater prospects of peace and progress.

Essentially, the Enlightenment was an international intellectual movement that was predominately French, although the movement was also influential in German, English, and American colonies.[1] This intellectual movement promoted certain values, among them intellectual and material progress, toleration, and critical reason.[2] The movement's major proponents included Montesquieu, Voltaire, and Diderot, of France; David Hume and John Locke, of England; and Thomas Jefferson, of the United States. These figures and others used critical reason to oppose not only traditional authority, both religious and political, but also the established social order on which these authorities were based. Intellectuals were opposed to theological politics, which based absolute power on a religious foundation.[3] The opposition to traditional authority that dominated in the Middle Ages was not unwarranted, for both Catholicism and Protestantism had become dogmatic and were often socially repressive.[4] Intellectuals expressed open skepticism about the value of these dogmatic systems and the theologies that supported them.[5]

Proponents of the Enlightenment believed that visible progress in civilization was possible. The rejection of some major tenets of Christianity, such as human fallenness, the ascetic Christian denial of the world, and the belief that human happiness is tied to the world to come, was viewed as the key to empowering human beings to facilitate that progress.[6] The freedom to exercise the gift of reason was critically important in bringing about human progress. Enlightenment figures, who drew inspiration from the classical ideas of Greeks and Romans, believed that the true form of things, such as the workings of the universe, the workings of the mind, and policies of effective government, could be discovered by the free exercise of reason. Human rationality was universal and could be developed by education. In Enlightenment thinking, human beings were viewed as free to the extent that their actions were governed by reason. Those actions governed by traditional authority, whether religious or political, were not deemed free. Freedom was represented by the exercise of one's intellect to make decisions about morality, religion, and politics.[7] Toleration, another important Enlightenment value, was necessary to ensure the social conditions required to enable people to use their own intellects to decide what they would believe.[8]

Humanity Comes of Age

As a result of this preoccupation with critical reason prompted by the Enlightenment, Europe became secularized and religion became a much more personalized and individualized affair.[9] As with any significant movement that brings about considerable social change, the Enlightenment's contribution to modernity had both positive and negative aspects with far-reaching consequences. On the positive side, the Enlightenment laid the intellectual foundation for the political revolutions that ushered in modernity in Europe and the United States. It formed the basis for liberal democratic societies.[10] It also contributed to advances in the physical and social sciences that would establish the prominence of the scientific worldview over the previous hegemony that Christianity had sustained since Constantine. On the negative side, certain views regarding the nature of humanity and its connection to a God who is actively engaged in the affairs of women and men emerged. These would lay, indirectly, a foundation that would salve the social conscience of those responsible for the support of slavery in the southern United States in the eighteenth

and nineteenth centuries and the savage persecution and genocide of the Jews under the Nazi regime.

The Autonomous Human

Rebellion against the stricture of religious tradition in this world
come of age brought about a change of view regarding human
nature and the relationship of humankind to God. The Christian
view of human beings recognized the dependence of humanity
before God its creator and its fallenness as a result of sin. Human
beings owed their existence to God and were incapable of partici-
pating in their own salvation. The view of humanity begun with
the Renaissance, strengthened by the Enlightenment, and rein-
forced in modernity is that human beings are autonomous and,
whether innately decent or innately power-hungry, responsible
for their own destiny. No longer was human dependence on God
emphasized. Rather, human beings were now viewed as responsible for themselves.[11]

Along with this view of human autonomy, modernity
upheld much confidence in the capacity of human reason to
solve human problems, to discover the nature of how the created order works, and to fulfill human potential to establish a
social order in which human beings could flourish. Not only
did reason, rather than revelation, have final authority for matters of faith and practice, but reason was elevated to the high-
est standard for judging all truth. The existence of God was
not completely denied, but the God of Enlightenment faith was
no longer understood as circumscribing the liberty of human
beings to act nor would this God invalidate the creative role of
humankind in history.[12]

The rise of the autonomous individual corresponds with the emergence of the commercial, bourgeois culture. This brought a sense of self-reliance, in which human history lies in the realm of human decisions rather than religious destiny and in which nature is viewed as an instrument rather than the master of human will.[13] The theological significance of modernity was found in the much greater difference between the biblical view and the modern view of humanity. The notion of the human creature subservient to God was no longer emphasized. Supreme confidence in the human capacity to reason brought much confidence in scientific method, technological advances, and a gradual shift from an agrarian society to urbanization. These swift changes would inspire much confidence in human ability to master the environment as well as the notion that human beings were steadily progressing toward moral maturity. These advances would thrust humanity into a curious moral dilemma that would reveal that human beings had transgressed God-given limits to what human beings could do. This dilemma would also reveal that overconfidence in human progress and a mistaken belief in human autonomy masked moral failures that modernity was blind to predict and incapable of avoiding without recognizing the need for grace.

A Fatal Paradox of Modernity

One great sentiment that emerged from modernity is the notion of the importance of liberty, the freedom to pursue a path that could ensure at least the possibility of a fulfilling, satisfying existence (happiness) in *this* life. No longer were people content with the rewards in a future life that were supposed to compensate for the reality of everyday hell in this one. The fatal paradox of modernity with respect to the vigorous pursuit of liberty for oneself is the vehement denial of freedom and fulfillment to *others*. This paradox, which seemed to trouble some of the greatest thinkers of the Enlightenment, became more apparent as first intellectuals and then policy makers became enamored with the scientific classification of human beings and the concept of race.

Race received growing attention during the Renaissance and throughout the Enlightenment period. Ideas about the inferiority of non-Europeans (based on Europeans' perceptions of non-Europeans in colonial accounts in the Americas and travel journals abroad) emerged alongside a growing scientific interest in the subject of race.[14] African American cultural critic Cornel West contends that the idea of white supremacy emerged partly because of the powers within the structure of modern discourse itself. These structures of modern discourse include the controlling metaphors, notions, categories, and norms that shape the predominant concepts of truth and knowledge in the modern West. The fusion of scientific investigation, Cartesian philosophy, classical aesthetics, and Western cultural ideals are some of the essential elements of modern discourse in the West that contributed to the emergence of white supremacist ideology.[15]

The starting point for the idea of white supremacy can be found in the classification categories and the descriptive, representational aims of natural history.[16] The second stage of modern racism arises from the popularity of phrenology (the reading of skulls) and physiognomy (the reading of faces).[17] These two initial stages provided intellectual legitimacy for the idea of white supremacy and were pervasive in the Enlightenment period. The validation of the idea of white supremacy in the intellectual and scientific sphere, coupled with the practical need to justify non-white domination, particularly in the early nineteenth century, is important in assessing the impact of white supremacist ideology on black people. Cornel West's point is well taken when he contends that "the everyday life of black people is shaped not simply by the exploitative (oligopolistic) capitalist system of production but also by cultural attitudes and sensibilities, including alienating ideals of beauty," and the stench of it can be detected in the air of postmodern times.[18]

In the eighteenth century, the study of race differences was in its infancy.[19] Perhaps more importantly, the absence of attention to racial differences in that century may have stemmed from the emphasis on universal reason in the Enlightenment. This emphasis on *universal* reason may have precluded, at least initially, considering the idea of innate character and intelligence because philosophers of the Age of Reason held a notion of universal progress. If, at birth, the mind of a child was not a tabula rasa, an empty receptacle, then education and environment could not be counted on to ensure the development of progeny to a completely reasonable and intelligent being.[20] Race theories would have challenged the optimism of the Enlightenment.

In general, eighteenth-century scientific opinion favored the idea of the potential intelligence and virtue of blacks and other nonwhites.[21] Eighteenth-century anthropology distinguished between species and varieties. Species were viewed as immutable prototypes, whereas varieties were members of a single species whose differences were attributable to such factors as climate and geography.[22] The fixity of species formed the basis for the classification system for all living organisms devised by Carolus Linnaeus. Linnaeus himself considered the races of humanity to be varieties rather than different species, and the differences seemed not to have been of much interest to him.[23]

On the other hand, George Louis Leclerc Buffon, one of the most influential authorities in natural history, did maintain that the white race is the norm and that it is to this race that one must look for the "real and natural color of man."[24] He also viewed the differences in terms of varieties rather than species; thus, race is not a constant but is predicated on such factors as climate, geography, nearness to the sea, diet, and social customs.[25] Blacks' pigmentation was attributed to the excessive heat of the tropical sun; however, it was thought that if they were imported to Europe, their descendents would gradually lighten in color over a period of generations.[26]

Johann Friedrich Blumenbach, who coined the word *Caucasian* to describe the white race, was a professor of medicine in Germany and had a lifelong interest in the study of race differences. He divided humankind into five varieties: Caucasian, Mongolian, Ethiopian, American, and Malay, corresponding to white, yellow, black, red, and brown race colors. He attributed differences in race to a combination of climate and other factors. He seems not to have had any antipathy against blacks or other nonwhite races but, rather, considered them potentially valuable members of society without hereditary taint.[27]

Rev. Samuel Stanhope Smith, a Presbyterian minister and professor of moral theology in the United States, wrote an ethnological treatise in 1787 that expressed the same optimism regarding the nonwhite races' capabilities as Buffon and Blumenbach. Smith deemed the differences in the races too numerous and complex develop an accurate system of classification. He believed that environment was all that precluded blacks and other nonwhite races from advancement. He asserted that if blacks "were perfectly free, enjoyed property, and were admitted to a liberal participation of the society, rank and privilege of their masters, they would change their African peculiarities much faster."[28] Yet, despite his optimism about black potential, Smith was said to be critical of blacks as he found them under slavery, though he was less harsh in his assessments than Thomas Jefferson.[29]

At this time, informed opinion tended to be on Smith's side in terms of optimism regarding the potential of blacks. Intellectual historian Thomas F. Gossett and other writers note the unease of some of the Founding Fathers about the contradiction between idealization of liberty and the enslavement of blacks by their slaveholders.[30]

Among those Founding Fathers afflicted in conscience was Thomas Jefferson, primary author of the Declaration of Independence, third president of the United States, and himself a slaveholder. However, despite Jefferson's ambivalence about the contradiction between liberty as an ideal and slaveholding as a practice, Jefferson's overall assessment of blacks—the victims of this contradiction—remained highly unflattering. This can be seen in his only full-length book, *Notes on the State of Virginia* (1787). In a discussion regarding the sustainability of a society in which blacks and whites were integrated as social equals, Jefferson made a number of disparaging observations in his comparison of blacks and whites, and he consistently ranked blacks as inferior to whites.

Aside from Jefferson's political considerations regarding integration, the moral and physical differences he noted between the two races are the most revealing.[31] He viewed skin color as the foundation for beauty and found the color of blacks offensive. Though uncertain of the physiological cause, he maintained that "glands of the skin" of blacks secreted a "strong and disagreeable odor." Morally, he felt that blacks were brave and "more adventuresome," but he maintained that this was probably due to their inability to anticipate the presence of danger. He felt that when blacks were confronted with danger, they were not as "cool" or "steady" as whites. He thought they were quite capable of physical ardor (or lust) but incapable of sexual tenderness and romantic affection.[32] Jefferson believed blacks to be incapable of deep or profound feelings or of a rich inner life, denying them an important dimension of humanness that betrays his conviction of their overall inferiority.[33] He wrote:

> [T]heir griefs are transient. Those numberless afflictions, which render it doubtful whether heaven has given life to us in mercy or in wrath, are less felt, and sooner forgotten with them. In general, their existence appears to participate more of sensation than reflection. . . . [In] reason [they are] much inferior . . . and in imagination they are dull, tasteless, and anomalous. . . . Never yet could I find that a black had uttered a thought above the level of plain narration; never see even an elementary trait of painting or sculpture. . . . Misery is often the parent of the most affecting touches in poetry— Among the blacks is misery enough . . . but no poetry. . . . Religion indeed has produced a Phyllis Whately [sic]; but it could not produce a poet. The compositions published under her name are below the dignity of criticism.[34]

This portrait of Jefferson is significant for it highlights the intellectual inconsistencies and moral ambivalence that characterize a number of key thinkers who embodied Enlightenment values and shaped Western thinking.

English physician Dr. Charles White shared a fascination regarding the differences in skin color that occupied Jefferson and others. Dr. White developed scientific arguments in favor of the idea of the multiple origins of the races. He held to the belief that there was a hierarchy, "a great chain of being," in which blacks occupy a different "station." This assessment seemed to rest squarely on the difference in physical characteristics between the races, in which the white race was viewed as the norm.[35] White denied any ulterior motives in formulating his theory of separate origins. He did not support the practice of slavery nor did he deem it appropriate that blacks should be stigmatized because they differed from whites as a species.[36]

The idea that blacks were a separate species was not generally supported in the eighteenth century, but some important thinkers of the Enlightenment and modernity tended to devalue blacks as human beings. John Locke, Voltaire, Montesquieu, David Hume, Charles White, Jean-Jacques Rousseau, and, later, Immanuel Kant and Georg Hegel were racists who questioned the full humanity of blacks and the justice of their right to freedom of full participation in a civilized society. They did so even as they fiercely espoused liberty and justice for themselves. For example, Montesquieu made remarks about blacks in his treatise "Spirit of the Laws" that suggest a disposition toward white supremacy.[37] In the essay "The People of America," Voltaire endorsed the idea of white supremacy unequivocally.[38] Hume was a major source of pro-slavery arguments and antiblack education propaganda.[39] Immanuel Kant denigrated the inner life and intellectual capacity of blacks in his essay "Observations on the Feeling of the Beautiful and the Sublime."[40] The arguments of Voltaire and Charles White were often repeated in nineteenth-century defenses of slavery.[41] The physical and social sciences, as well as philosophy, were used to defend the notion of the innate inferiority of blacks.

In the meantime, as the new "science" of race began to develop under the impetus of advances in anthropology and philology,[42] pseudoscientific racialism provided the fuel for secular anti-Semitism. Arthur de Gobineau, a historian, contended that the racial question would overshadow all other problems of history, that it held the key to all of them, and that the inequality of the races would be enough to explain their destiny. In a perverse sense, his observation proved prophetic. The idea of race as the determinant of the rise and fall of civilizations appeared among the German philologists and ethnologists and philosophers, who believed that social degeneration came from racial degeneration as well as from racial mixture, which dissipated the pure racial blood and brought on mediocrity and decline.[43]

White Supremacy and Anti-Semitism as Forms of Racism

What then is the link between white supremacy and anti-Semitism? Although the religious element and underpinnings remain a factor in anti-Semitism, the nineteenth century marks a substantial shift in the character and tone of anti-Judaism and the corresponding treatment of Jews. By the first half of the nineteenth century, democratic ideals spread, bringing citizenship and full equality to Jews in Western Europe. With the exception of Russia, country after country repealed anti-Jewish legislation and restrictions. However, new, secular justifications for anti-Judaism emerged to replace the Christian anti-Semitism of the past. With the new justifications, a new term—"Anti-Semitism"[44]—was coined to encompass anti-Jewish attitudes and behaviors based on racial and pseudoscientific theories.[45]

By the second half of the nineteenth century, harassment, insults, and hostility were part of the daily experience of Jewish men, women, and children. Whereas formerly Jews might have expected some relief from harassment through assimilation and even conversion to Christianity, such tactics of self-preservation were no longer deterrents to discrimination. Conjecture based on racial theories determined that the characteristics or, more precisely, the caricatures ascribed to Jews—that they were vile, conspiratorial, greedy, and subhuman—were believed to be innate and immutable.[46] Because these so-called characteristics were thought to be genetic and permanent, persecution and hatred of the Jews were viewed now as not only justified but also respectable. By the twentieth century, the racial developments of the previous century would be combined with the nationalistic fervor of the new century. With the rise of the Nazis, blood and soil and racial ideologies would divinize the Aryan race while at the same time dehumanizing Jews, making the Nazi extermination of the latter an inevitable and "logical" consequence.

On the basis of how anti-Semitism became racialized in nineteenth-century Europe, acquiring many of the characteristics of the term *race* as it applied to whites and blacks in the United States, I maintain that secularized, racial anti-Semitism is another form of racism that operates in similar ways to other forms of racism. In light of how blacks and Jews were caricatured, persecuted, and restricted from the economic, social, and political realms of their respective societies, a comprehensive definition of the term *racism* seems warranted.[47] Racism, for our purposes, is defined as follows: *Racism is hatred, hostility, contempt, ill will, condescension, or prejudice against a certain group on the basis of race.*

A full elaboration of the term and how it functions is in order. Racism includes the absence of "human feeling" toward the targeted group and the denial of the group members' full humanity, by attitude or actions, and/or their right to participate as full human beings in society. Racism calls for the exclusion of, or the desire to exclude, the targeted population from full participation within a society. It often involves social, economic, and political maltreatment toward those classified as a particular race. It involves blatant and subtle attempts to limit their freedom and intercourse in society. It manifests itself as an ideology of racial inferiority but includes discourse, conduct, customs, social policies, and even legislation to sustain the oppression of those deemed inferior in status. The physical, linguistic, ethnic, or cultural differences that the "inferior" race possesses (or is perceived to possess) are viewed as impediments to social interaction with the in-group. Moreover, the differences are viewed as a justification for refusing to recognize and honor the full humanity of the out-group. (Racism can exist in the oppressed or the powerless, but its impact is most egregious when those with economic, social, and political power use their resources to withhold services or impede or preclude the full participation of those in the despised group.) What is salient about racism is the contempt and disregard for the welfare of certain people primarily *because of their race.*[48]

This rather comprehensive definition indicates that racism can operate as a fully encompassing ideology. In the case of white supremacy and anti-Semitism, both have functioned as all-encompassing, dehumanizing ideologies of death. They are egregious examples of the sin of defacement. This all-encompassing aspect of racism further justifies examining white supremacy and anti-Semitism together. (In chapter 5, we will examine more fully the ways in which both white supremacy and anti-Semitism functioned as lethal ideologies and consider why these ideologies are problematic from a Christian theological perspective.)

Communal Defacement as a Blight on Modernity

Earlier in this chapter, I identified several elements of the project of modernity that contributed to the shift in tone in black and Jewish antipathies in the nineteenth and twentieth centuries. The Age of Reason marked the historical moment in which Western humanity understood itself as no longer under the tutelage of religious or political authority. This period marked the moment in which Europeans and North Americans celebrated the autonomy of human beings. Humanity had come of age, and the faculty of reason was elevated as the final arbiter for judging the world and all things in it. The chief end of human beings was no longer the glorification of God; rather, it was the attainment of the good things of life, liberty (for some), and the pursuit of happiness here on earth. The philosophical tenets of the Enlightenment untied humanity from its theological moorings because of the corruption of religious and political authorities. Enlightenment thinkers viewed this detachment as a way to escape from the oppressive and coercive tethers of corrupt church and state authorities.

However, the leading Enlightenment figures did not reckon with the reality and the depth of sin from which human beings cannot overcome without divine grace. Too much confidence was placed in the faculty of reason to guide human beings on matters governing human conduct, individually and corporately. Human

reason was treated as infallible, and the pretensions of this infallible authority placed Western human beings in the position of sole
arbiter of morality and sole determiner of human destiny. Supreme
confidence in the notion that human beings could be autonomous
from God constituted hubris that rendered Western humanity
idolatrous. The blindness that accompanies idolatry obscured just
how tragically human beings could be led astray. The profound
irony is that an ideology of enlightenment, which valorized liberty
and promoted freedom at great human cost, served as the corner-
stone for societies that could justify the perpetual enslavement of
one group in the human family and attempt the annihilation of
another group. Modernity marks the historical moment in which
corporate defacement became embedded into the structures and
systems of two societies through ideologies of death. ■

White Supremacy and Racial Anti-Semitism: Ideologies of Death

5

I longed to die, and escape from the hands of my tormentors; but even the wretched privilege of destroying myself was denied me; for I could not shake off my chains.

—CHARLES BALL

Today I realize that it would have been better if they had killed us all. . . . It would have been more humane.

—MIRIAM KORBER

The previous chapter established that the historical meeting place for racial anti-Semitism and white supremacy was modernity. Certain tenets of the Enlightenment project provided the philosophical grounding by which anti-Semitism and white supremacy became corporate expressions of communal defacement. In turn, these expressions of communal defacement became embedded in the economic, social, and political systems and structures of their respective societies. They became "ideologies of death." The nature of this death was sometimes physical, sometimes spiritual, but always psychical. I take seriously the notion that ideologies can be lethal. In this chapter, I will define what ideologies are, explain how they function, and articulate the specific ways in which white supremacy and anti-Semitism served as ideologies of death.

In theological circles, there has been a long-standing debate regarding the term *ideology*.[1] The views of two contemporary theologians—Juan Luis Segundo and Allan A. Boesak—exemplify the two poles of this debate. Segundo, a Latin American liberation theologian, disagrees with the "popular" tendency to make a radical distinction between those who have "faith" and those who structure their lives around an "ideology."[2] He believes that formulating a dichotomy such as "faith vs. ideology" is incorrect and argues for a different understanding of both terms. Segundo maintains that both "faith" and "ideology" are universal dimensions of human experience. Faith (adult faith, specifically) is the human dimension that constitutes a structure of meaning in a person's life. Faith is a structure of values that informs us about not only what we ought to do but also how we perceive reality, *whether religion is involved or not.* Faith enables us to see things in one particular way rather than *another equally valid way.* Ideology is a second dimension of human experience. It is composed of *all* systems of means, natural or artificial, that are used to attain a particular end or goal. Ideology represents a vision of how things should be, without any reference to meaning or value, because ideology stands outside of values.[3]

Given these definitions of faith and ideology, Segundo argues that it is erroneous to view these two terms as oppositional because ideology does not determine either the meaning-structure or the values-structure of a human life. On the contrary, human beings seek methods to pursue particular goals in terms of the values they appreciate most. Thus, no one can replace faith with ideology in seeking to determine the basic values of one's life. For Segundo, ideology is a function of, and determined by, one's faith or value system. The significance of his insistence that faith is not necessarily a religious term correlates with his conviction that all of us are governed by the values we hold dear, whether those values are shaped by a particular religious tradition or not. As human beings, we are governed by the values we adopt, and those values come to us through various inherited traditions that are not necessarily religious in origin. According to Segundo, the terms *faith* and *ideology* are anthropological (that is, part of being a human being) and *not* spiritual or religious. Faith and ideology express part of what it means, by nature, to be human.

In light of Segundo's definitions, faith and ideology are complementary, not oppositional. They are two dimensions of the human person that work together. A particular ideology is considered useful to the degree that it helps realize a goal that has been shaped by the values a person holds dear. To the degree that an ideology successfully serves faith, it remains part of a person's belief system. However, should the ideology prove unserviceable given the values adopted by the individual, the ideology will be revised or else the "faith" will be altered. Segundo contends that theology is always ideological. He asserts that it is "naïve" to maintain that theology should never be ideological, as though the word of God is applied to human realities inside an antiseptic laboratory that is completely immune to the ideological tendencies and struggles of the present day.[4] Because theology is inherently contextual, the task of theological reflection should not be approached by attempting to obscure or hide behind a particular social structure; rather, one should acknowledge the origins of such reflection and submit to the kind of self-questioning and continual reinterpretation of reality. Since all theology is ideological, Segundo contends, we must be conscious of the *particular* ideology that governs our discourse. Denial of the presence of ideology, or obscuring it, does not render theology free of ideology; rather, the ignorance of it ensures that a non-liberating ideology will prevail.

There is much to commend in Segundo's discussion about recognizing that theological reflection never occurs in a vacuum but, rather, always arises out of a particular context. He is correct when he maintains that the theologian is always engaged in theological reflection from a particular social location, that the theologian comes from a particular economic class and has had particular advantages that arise out of certain educational opportunities. Out of that particular location, with its own social, economic, and political interests, the theologian engages his or her religious tradition. This context undoubtedly shapes the theologian's perception of reality. This embeddedness in social location is unavoidable and is part of being an embodied person. All of the above is true.

However, as valuable as Segundo's insight might be with regard to the significance of recognizing one's embeddedness in a particular social location, which undoubtedly shapes one's perception of reality, his cut-and-dried definitions of faith and ideology are problematic. Although he maintains that faith and ideology are anthropological dimensions of the human being, his discussion of them is not directed by an understanding of the human being as a creature *coram Deo*, as a being who lives *before God*. This comes to light most clearly when he asserts that faith is the anthropological dimension that constitutes a structure of meaning in the human person that is present and operative whether religion is involved or not.

I would argue that, while a person may or may not espouse a particular religious tradition, we cannot remove the discussion of faith outside the realm of religion if we affirm that human beings live their lives *coram Deo*. To affirm humanity as living *coram Deo* is to assert that no area of our lives is out of the bounds of God's concern. This is true whether or not a person chooses to recognize this creaturely reality. Given Segundo's definition of faith, which informs us about not only what we ought to do but also how we perceive reality, he is speaking about faith in *religious* terms, if we, as theologians, understand that human beings live their lives *coram Deo*. Thus, the religious content of the concept of faith, even as Segundo defines the term, is not abrogated by a person's decision not to subscribe to a particular religious tradition, for Segundo is right when he speaks about faith as an anthropological dimension of human existence. Human beings place their trust in something or someone or in God. The *real* theological issue, however, is whether one places his or her faith in God or in something less than God. Additionally, Segundo errs in his discussion of faith and ideology by his rendering of *ideology* as a neutral term, devoid of meaning and structure—as simply the dimension that provides the structure to support the living out of faith. More will be said regarding this concern later in this chapter.

In contrast to Segundo, black South African theologian Allan Boesak upholds an antithetical relationship between faith and ideology, or, more precisely, between Christian theology and ideology. Boesak is aware that there are various ways of understanding ideology. In a positive sense, ideology can be understood as a system of ideas, a blueprint, or a plan to reach certain goals in the sociopolitical field. This view is consistent with the way Segundo has chosen to define ideology, seeking to use the term in a way consistent with its etymological origin. But the term *ideology* has evolved, especially through the work of Karl Marx, who saw ideology as a pathological form of human knowledge estranged from the real processes of life, masking the extent of human maladjustment and alienation.[5] Marx viewed ideology as a way of conceiving the world that conceals the economic and material origin of enslavement and alienation.[6] Others, including Karl Mannheim, maintain that ideologies may transcend reality but they always justify the status quo.[7] As a system, ideology consolidates the existing power structure by offering an idealization of either the present or the future.[8] Although cognizant of moves within the theological community to restore use of the term *ideology* in a way consistent with its etymological origin, Boesak prefers to use the term in its previous pejorative sense. This decision is strengthened by the power of the phenomenological description of the way ideology functions in particular contexts. (It is important to note that when Boesak discussed his view of ideology, he did so in the context of apartheid in South Africa.)

Boesak employs five criteria formulated by Albert Stüttgen to explain how ideologies actually function.[9] First, an ideology makes claims of absoluteness and exclusivity, constituting a comprehensive pretension to know all of reality. Evident will be an unwillingness to allow those claims to be corrected because of a certainty that the claims could never be wrong. Second, a complete schism with the world of real, daily experiences exists. The ideology will remain unaffected by the counter-experiences of others or the results of scientific research. Third, the ideology resides within a closed, isolated, fossilized system of ideas with no room for change. Fourth, the ideology lives on presuppositions that are purposely kept unclear and vague. Fifth, the ideology needs prejudices and clichés to survive.

With Stüttgen's criteria in mind, Boesak defines ideology as an idea or system of ideas—a doctrine or theory or system of doctrines or theories used to justify and perpetuate existing structures of injustice.[10] Ideology constitutes not only theory but praxis, and the self-justifying character of an ideology is usually hidden from the group using the ideology. Moreover, a relationship exists between the ideology and the sociopolitical reality in which power is legitimated. Boesak's definition of ideology captures the theologically pathological nature of the term in a way that Juan Luis Segundo does not. Boesak's discussion of ideology arises out of a particular context, and his use of Albert Stüttgen's criteria gives definite shape and contour to the term. It is a fully encompassing definition in that he refuses to limit ideology to a theory or set of ideas alone but recognizes that ideology also includes actions or practices that are inextricably related to the system of ideas in question. Power is also an important variable in the equation to the degree that sociopolitical power affects the consequences associated with an ideology.

In addition to all of the above factors, Boesak's definition of ideology aids our discussion of black slavery and the Holocaust because it implies that there is a core of beliefs and praxes associated with right relationships within a community from which an ideology will deviate and thus undermine those right relationships.

For these reasons, his definition of ideology has much to commend it.

With elements of both Segundo's and Boesak's discussion of the relationship of faith to ideology in mind, we will craft an understanding of the two terms as they relate to the role of ideology in white supremacy and anti-Semitism. From Segundo, we recognize a connection between faith and ideology. Segundo believes the two dimensions are complementary. Boesak, however, regards them as oppositional, in light of his appropriation of Albert Stüttgen's criteria. For our purposes, we will treat the two terms as oppositional, based not only on Stüttgen's five criteria but also on a sixth one that should be added in light of our discussion of white supremacy and anti-Semitism: *The ideology masks or obscures the real nature of its goals within society.* This sixth criterion will prove particularly relevant as we look at the ways that the ideology of white supremacy functioned in the context of slavery and its legacy here in the United States and the way the ideology of anti-Semitism functioned in the context of Germany in the 1930s and 1940s.

With regard to Segundo's belief that ideology constitutes a vision of reality and, more importantly, that ideology has to do with all systems of means, natural or artificial, used to attain a particular end or goal, we agree that ideologies can serve that function. However, we deny that "ideologies" are neutral in terms of meanings and values, for in light of Albert Stüttgen's criteria, and the sixth one I have added, ideologies connect to *idolatry* rather than to faith proper. Earlier, we noted that human beings subscribe to faith in either something or someone or in God. Even if a person claims to be an atheist, he or she places his or her trust in something or someone other than God. Therefore, we understand faith to be a theological category, and not simply an anthropological category, because human beings are creatures that live *coram Deo*, before God, whether they recognize this reality of human existence or not. For our purposes, we define faith in the following way: Faith is *fiducia*, or complete trust, in God to be faithful to the divine promises made to support, sustain, and uphold us in God's care from cradle to grave according to divine will and mercy.[11]

Here we see that faith is something on which we stake our lives. We measure the quality of our life by the object of faith. This object will shape our outlook on economic, social, and political matters. It will even "trump" our "interests" to remain the guiding force of our existence. It even trumps "reason." We will go to extraordinary lengths to keep our allegiance with this God. Our minds will become closed to evidence that our assessment of the out-group is wrong. Not even will the gospel prevail over this allegiance. Defacement of others becomes a crucial measure by which we remain "faithful" to our God.

This definition reflects that the nature of faith is complete trust in God to care for us as God sees fit insofar as we belong to God as one of God's creatures. Whatever becomes of us, however we proceed in life, our existence is sustained by the hand of God. Insofar as we are creatures who live *coram Deo* all the days of our lives, our trust or faith can only be properly placed in God. Praxis, or committed action, to live faithfully before God then arises out of trust in God's faithfulness and mercy to sustain us. The complementary relationship to faith, therefore, is praxis. On the other hand, idolatry is antithetical to faith, because it is trust in something or someone *other than God*. All systems, plans, and visions that proceed from trust or faith in anything or anyone other than God are ideology, not praxis, because ideology constitutes a blueprint or vision or plan based on faith in something other than God, which is treated as though it were God. Thus, the relationship between idolatry and ideology is analogous to the relationship between faith and praxis. Theologically, there is no complementary relationship between faith and ideology, as Segundo maintains. Ideology arises out of idolatry, not out of a neutral "faith," because, properly speaking, faith is trust in God and not simply "that which provides meaning and value."

Given our understanding of ideology, we can turn our discussion now to how ideology relates to white supremacy and anti-Semitism and why it is that we can speak, theologically, about them as "ideologies of death." We have noted previously that white supremacy and anti-Semitism are forms of racialism. Theologically, racialism, in the context of both blacks and Jews, is a form of idolatry—a rival "faith." The following discussion will explain how this is so.

Racialism: A Rival "Faith"

In 1962, African American Christian ethicist George D. Kelsey published a study on racism titled *Racism and the Christian Understanding of Man*. In this work, Kelsey highlighted the modern dimensions of racism as he carefully distinguished between it and the phenomenon of ethnocentrism, which has a long history in human experience. Kelsey observed, as we have already demonstrated, that racial alienation is a modern phenomenon. Gradually, in modernity, the basis for the division of in-group and out-group shifted from religious superiority to racial superiority. Modern racism emerged as somewhat of an afterthought—a consequence of the ideological justification of European political and economic domination over people of color. Although modern racism emerged as a consequence of particular economic and political circumstances, Kelsey correctly stressed that racism developed as an independent phenomenon. It has morphed into a complete system of meaning and value in itself that has shaped every institution in some societies.

What renders Kelsey's analysis so relevant for our purposes is that he understood this shift from ethnocentrism to an ideology of pervasive proportions in fundamentally *theological* terms.[12] Racism is a false "faith," a pseudo-faith that rivals Christianity, because it represents a search for meaning. Kelsey commented on the idolatrous character of this "faith":

> The fact that racism exists alongside other faiths does not make it any less a faith. Rather, this fact is testimony to the reality of polytheism in the modern age. In its maturity, racism is not a mere ideology that a political demagogue may be expected to affirm or deny, depending upon the political situation in which he finds himself. Racism is a search for meaning. The devotee of the racist faith is as certainly seeking self-identity in his acts of self-exaltation and his self-deifying pronouncements as he is seeking to nullify the selfhood of members of outraces by acts of deprivation and words of vilification.[13]

This faith character of racism makes it the "final and complete form of human alienation." Moreover, "it is the prototype of all human alienation." This assessment is defended by Kelsey's assertion that racism is the one form of human conflict that divides human beings *as human beings*. The racist glorifies in his or her own being and rejects members of the out-race precisely because of their being.[14] Kelsey's critique of racism recognizes not only that the self-deification of the "in-race" is a theological problem but that the racist also posits a pejorative judgment concerning the action of God. Because racism assumes that some segments of humanity are defective in their essential being, and since Christianity affirms that all being is from the hand of God, "racism alone among the idolatries calls into question the divine creative action." God has made an error in bringing the out-races into being.[15] Kelsey concludes that racism is a *theological* error, rather than an anthropological one.[16] Either blacks are victims of a "double fall" (which includes not only the initial fall of all humanity recorded in Genesis 3 but also a second fall involving blacks alone) or blacks share not only in the universal condemnation of the human race in Adam but also bear an *added* condemnation of God in a special, racial fall.[17] Either way, their subordinate status is justified and serves as the explanation of blacks' secondary place in society.

Although Kelsey's analysis was tied to the issue of race in the United States, he perceived that the plight of Jews as victims of racialized anti-Semitism was clearly analogous, and I maintain that he is correct on this issue.[18] By appropriating a definition derived from the work of Ruth Benedict, Kelsey identified the ways in which the faith character of racism can be disclosed in its facets, revealing the theological character of racism: "[It is] the *dogma* that one ethnic group is condemned by Nature to hereditary inferiority and another group is destined to hereditary superiority. It is the *dogma* that the hope of civilization depends upon eliminating some races and keeping others pure. It is the *dogma* that one race has carried progress throughout human history and can alone ensure future progress."[19]

Clearly, this understanding of racism pertains to the ideology of racial anti-Semitism as it functioned with respect to European Jews in the 1930s and 1940s. One aspect of this racialized anti-Semitism can be seen in the concept of the German Volk. Ernst Arndt, a poet and pamphleteer, and his disciple Friedrich Jahn, a fierce German patriot, are credited with developing the concept of the Volk in the nineteenth century. The term *Volk* is loosely translated as "a people," but it encompasses a more transcendent quality than merely "people." It can signify the union of a group of people with a transcendental "essence" or "nature" or "mythos."[20] The significance of the concept of Volk cannot be overestimated in terms of the motivations governing the appeal of Adolf Hitler's nationalist socialist program as a means of enabling Germany to recover its nationalistic pride following the devastating humiliations of post–World War I sanctions. Preoccupation with the Volk and its significance for the establishment of Germany and its people can be seen in a lecture delivered in 1937 by Paul Althaus, one of Germany's premier theologians in the 1920s and 1930s and an intellectual captivated by national socialist ideology:

As a creation of God, the *Volk* is a law of our life. . . . We are responsible for the inheritance, the blood inheritance and the spiritual inheritance, for *Bios* and *Nomos*, that it be preserved in its distinctive style and authenticity. We are unconditionally bound to faithfulness, to responsibility, so that the life of the *Volk* as it has come down to us not be contaminated or weakened through our fault. We are bound to stand up for the life of our *Volk*, even to the point of risking our own life.[21]

Althaus would continue, giving a clear indication of the importance of the Volk in his system of values: "Our life in our *Volk* is not our eternal life; but we have no eternal life if we do not live for our *Volk*. This is not a question of the absolute value of the *Volk*, but of our absolute obligation to the *Volk*."[22]

Jahn contended that the Volk needed a state to house its soul and provide the means for its preservation, and the German state was designed to serve the purpose—to preserve the Volk and to be the vehicle to exercise its purpose.[23] Jews were automatically precluded from membership in the Volk. In fact, they were viewed as the enemy of the Volk as they could not be members of the Christian state because they were loyal to their own "state within a state."[24] The effect of this was to render Jews perpetual aliens in Germany. The German became the embodiment not only of the natural man but of Germanic man; the Jew became his antagonist—the embodiment of the urban man, the man of civilization.[25]

The logic of racism is genocide. Because that which renders an out-race objectionable is fundamental to who they are, the only way to remove that which is objectionable is to eliminate the offending out-race. Since who the Jews were could not be altered or changed, the "final solution" of Hitler was deemed necessary for the salvation of the Third Reich. Interestingly enough, with regard to African Americans in the United States, genocide seems not to have been seriously considered by the mainstream—perhaps because their uncompensated labor was viewed as a distinct economic advantage to the white in-race. Nevertheless, extermination of an out-race is *always* a possibility.

The Plight of African Americans and the Ideology of White Supremacy

The sin of defacement, in its corporate or communal expression, can become embedded into legislation and social policies that make it legal and the natural order of things to keep minorities from the opportunities needed to participate effectively in national life. The sin of defacement is probably most visible when one group in a society decides that another group is not fit to live.

As we look at the plight of African Americans from slavery to the modern civil rights movement of the 1950s and 1960s, we can see how white supremacy functioned as an ideology of death—if not always physical then psychically and spiritually. Whites of the United States enforced the ideology of white supremacy through the use of the law. In the late eighteenth and early nineteenth centuries, once the colonies secured their own independence from England, the lower South enacted new, stringent laws known as the Slave Codes.

These laws covered all aspects of the life of the slave. Although they varied from state to state, they were all designed to establish that slaves were not persons but property. The laws were intended to ensure that the slaves were subordinated sufficiently to ensure maximum discipline and work. Slaves had no standing in the courts—for example, they could not sue, they could not offer testimony except against another slave or free black, and their oath was not binding. They could not make contracts, though some could have certain types of personal property. Slaves could not strike a white person, even in self-defense. The killing of a slave was rarely punished. The rape of a female slave was viewed as "trespassing," not as a sexual assault. Slaves could not leave the plantation without authorization. If a white person found a slave away from the plantation without permission, he could turn the slave over to public officials. Slaves could not own firearms. They could not hire themselves out without permission or buy and sell goods. Blacks could not assemble together without the presence of a white person. These restrictions were tightened whenever there were slave revolts.[26] The restrictions upon free blacks in the North were sometimes nearly as oppressive as they were to blacks who were enslaved. For most quasi-free blacks, existence was often bleak because of the pervasive antipathy toward blacks.

The ideology of white supremacy was also maintained through the use of terror. With the advent of the Radical Reconstruction period (1863–77), violence against blacks escalated. Disenfranchisement of blacks soon followed their economic subjugation after Reconstruction.[27] Once northern liberalism acquiesced to the Compromise of 1877, which moved toward some degree of political reconciliation between the North and South, there was a retreat from resistance to racism.[28] Southern politicians, well-steeped in the tradition of white supremacy, now found themselves with support abroad from biologists, sociologists, anthropologists, historians, novelists, and journalists, adding a dimension of acceptability and popularity to racism.[29]

Poll taxes, ownership of property, and literacy qualifications became part of the standard devices for disenfranchisement of blacks.[30] By 1870, nearly every southern state saw the entrenchment of not only the Ku Klux Klan but other similar organizations, such as the Knights of the White Camelia and the White Brotherhood, all of which wrought a reign of terror to blacks.[31] Through the late nineteenth century and well into the twentieth century, despite their emancipation, blacks lived through demoralizing poverty, the terror of lynching, and systematic exclusion from the economic, social, and political processes of the United States. The Ku Klux Klan and other bands of white men roamed the South at night terrorizing blacks.[32] Thousands of blacks were murdered throughout the South by the Klan during Reconstruction; many were beaten and driven from the land, despite legislation enacted by Congress in 1870 and 1871.

The Compromise of 1877 spelled the end of Reconstruction, and millions of black citizens lost their civil rights.[33] Jim Crow, the racial rules of the South, became prevalent in every southern state.[34] "White" and "colored" signs went up; trains, buses, barbershops, schools, and other public places were segregated by law.[35] During Reconstruction, the Thirteenth Amendment prohibited slavery everywhere in the United States, and the Fourteenth Amendment guaranteed the civil liberties of blacks. The Fifteenth Amendment secured their right to vote, and civil rights legislation was passed. Yet, with the end of Reconstruction, blacks would not profit from these constitutional gains.[36]

The ideology of white supremacy was also maintained through a system of economic, social, and political domination by custom and deliberate acts of discrimination. By the 1950s, southern whites had established a threefold system of domination over blacks, which made life demeaning for blacks and upheld white privilege. This system encompassed economic, social, and political degradation and domination. Economically, blacks were stuck in low-paying jobs; politically, they suffered systematic exclusion from the political process; and socially, they were denied freedom of movement and full participation in normal social life. This system of domination was supported by legislation and enforced by local and state governments.[37]

In light of Albert Stüttgen's five criteria, as well as the sixth criterion I added earlier in this chapter, we can see how white supremacy functioned as a lethal ideology. The comprehensive domination of African Americans, particularly in the South, claimed an absoluteness and exclusivity that did not allow for exceptions to its perception of blacks as a group inferior to whites and, therefore, without claim to the rights and privileges afforded to whites. White supremacy also claimed an absoluteness and exclusivity with regard to its belief about the "proper" relationship between blacks and whites.[38] We can also say that there was an unwillingness to allow those claims to be corrected because of a certainty that the claims could never be wrong.

Whites who had little or no dealings with blacks (for example, in some locations in the North) maintained just as strong antipathy, hostility, and disparagement toward blacks as that of whites in the South. Where daily experience with blacks occurred, whites tended to dismiss instances where their perceptions of the intelligence, character, and capabilities of blacks were inconsistent with reality. White supremacy operated within a closed, isolated, fossilized system of ideas with no room for change. Stereotypes and caricatures of black culture, life, language, and customs were needed to keep white supremacy alive. Elaborate justifications for slavery were given when humanitarians from the North began to agitate for emancipation, including the need to evangelize slaves, the need to colonize free blacks to Africa, the innate inferiority of blacks to govern themselves, and the notion of the "happy" slave. These justifications and others masked the reality that slavery and the system of economic, social, and political domination were deeply oppressive and inherently dehumanizing. The ideology of white supremacy wrought untold misery to a population whose only crime was its designation as an inferior race.

The ideology of white supremacy sustained itself long past the end of slavery. Yet, despite the prolonged season of oppression, abuse, and dehumanization, it was the grace of their human dignity that enabled blacks to resist in ways that ensured their survival, however truncated, harsh, and problematic it was. Although blacks did not experience wholesale genocide under the ideology of white supremacy, European Jewry would know the bitter taste of attempted extermination by the hand of Adolf Hitler's Nazi regime.

Jews of Europe and the Ideology of German Anti-Semitism, 1933–1945

In the context of Germany in the 1930s and 1940s, the embeddedness of corporate defacement in economic, social, and political structures can be seen just as much as or even more clearly than in the American South. With Hitler's rise to power in the early 1930s, government legislation was enacted that sanctioned the violence already being perpetrated against the Jews. It began with the elimination of Jews from government service and public life. The first anti-Jewish law of the Third Reich was enacted in April 1933. Before the end of World War II, four hundred laws and decrees were enacted, decrees that would lead to the near destruction of European Jewry. The first decree, "Law for the Restoration of the Professional Civil Service," authorized the elimination of both Jews and political opponents of the Nazi regime from the civil service. A companion law promulgated at the same time canceled the admission to the bar of lawyers of non-Aryan descent and denied permission to those already admitted to practice law. In quick succession, similar laws excluded Jews from posts as lay assessors, jurors, commercial judges, patent lawyers, panel physicians in state socio-insurance institutions, and dentists and dental technicians associated with institutions.[39] A succession of additional laws led to the eventual exclusion of Jews from public life, government, culture, and the professions.[40]

In addition to laws designed to exclude Jewish men and women from meaningful participation in German society, a number of laws were enacted that would systematically dehumanize and legally criminalize Jewish personhood in Germany. The Aryan paragraph, promulgated on April 11, 1933, defined a non-Aryan as anyone "descended from non-Aryan, especially Jewish, parents or grandparents." A person was non-Aryan even if only one parent or grandparent was non-Aryan. This was especially true if that parent or grandparent was Jewish. Civil servants were required to prove that they were Aryans through the submission of a birth certificate and the marriage certificate of the parents.[41]

Two years later, in 1935, new anti-Jewish laws, the Nuremberg Laws, were adopted unanimously by the Reichstag. These laws legitimized racist anti-Semitism and turned the "purity of German blood" into a legal category. They forbade marriage and extramarital relations between Germans and Jews and also disenfranchised those "subjects" or "nationals" of Germany who were not of Jewish blood.[42]

Moreover, many institutions would emerge as watchdogs of racial breeding and purification.[43] Preserving the racial purity of Germany ("positive eugenics") was an important aspect of racial policy in National Socialist legislation to exclude Jewish "impurity."[44] Anti-Jewish legislation set the Jews apart from Germans legally, politically, and socially—removing the Jews from state protection. The Nuremberg Laws brought to completion the disenfranchisement of the Jews of Germany.[45]

The night of November 9–10, 1938, known as *Kristallnacht* ("Crystal Night," or "the night of broken glass"), was the most violent public display of anti-Semitism in modern German history.[46] The pogrom, sparked by the killing of a German diplomat in Paris by a young Polish Jew whose family had been expelled from Germany and denied reentry into Poland, was organized by the German government and Nazi organizations and supported by the mobs.[47] The pogrom of 1938 rivaled those associated with czarist Russia.[48] Kristallnacht marked a watershed on Hitler's path to the "final solution."[49] It involved the seizure of Jewish property and the acceleration of the total exclusion of Jews from the Germany economy. The violence of the SS (Schutzstaffel) was unleashed without restraint.[50] "Every synagogue in Germany was burnt down or demolished and over 30,000 Jewish men were seized and sent to concentration camps. Many Jewish businesses were destroyed and several hundred Jews were murdered or severely wounded."[51] The Nazis stepped up their persecution of Jews from 1938 forward.[52]

The logical conclusion of the racial anti-Semitism legalized in Nazi Germany was extermination of this population of men, women, and children who were viewed as a pronounced threat to the German vision of renewed glory. However, historians have failed to uncover any written order by Adolf Hitler to eliminate the Jews. Nevertheless, research indicates that the decision to annihilate the Jews was probably reached after December 18, 1940, when Hitler issued the first directive for operation Barbarossa, and before March 1, 1941.[53] Commitment to rid Europe of the Jewish population would take precedence over even military exigencies, as World War II progressed.[54]

While the Jews were alive, their labor was extracted without reward or mercy. After their deportation, the Germans expropriated their remaining goods.[55] The deported Jews were sent to Auschwitz, Belzec, Ghelmno, Majdanek, Sobibor, and Tremblinka. Ten percent—the fittest looking—were selected for work. The remaining men, women, and children were sent to the gas chambers. They were made to undress, and the hair of the women and girls was cut. They were hurried to the gas chambers through a phalanx of whips, sticks, or guns. The chambers were said to be showers; the Jews were rammed in, and the gassing lasted from ten to thirty minutes. To make room for more victims, the dead were tossed out "blue, wet with sweat and urine, the legs covered with feces and menstrual blood." Later, the bodies were burned, either in open air or in crematoria.[56] The Nazi death camps were liberated in the spring of 1945, and Adolf Hitler and a few of his most trusted advisors took their own lives in late April 1945, putting an end to the official campaign to rid the world of Jews.

In light of Albert Stüttgen's five criteria, as well as the sixth criterion I added, we can see how racial anti-Semitism functioned as a lethal ideology. The systematic erasure of Jews from common life in Germany, through laws and customs designed to isolate them from the German Volk, claimed an absoluteness and exclusivity that did not allow for exceptions to its perception of Jews as not only inferior but dangerous to the well-being of German people. Therefore, they were perceived as a group who had no claim to the rights and privileges afforded to those who were of the "Aryan" race.

Racial anti-Semitism also claimed an absoluteness and exclusivity regarding its belief about the "proper" relationship between Aryans and non-Aryans, especially Jews. In light of the deliberate and calculating way in which Nazification of Germany and parts of Europe operated, there was an unwillingness on the part of powerful supporters of Nazism to allow the correction of claims about the Jews because of an almost religious certainty that the claims could never be wrong. The implementation of anti-Jewish legislation and policies were an attempt to hermetically seal the Third Reich and its supporters from "contamination" by the Jews. The death camps, an implementation of the "final solution," clearly reflected that the Nazis were unlikely to entertain any room for change in their view of Jews. Stereotypes and caricatures of Jewish religion, culture, life, character, and customs were kept alive by an elaborate propaganda machine presided over by the minister of propaganda, George Goebbels, in order to encourage and sustain racial anti-Semitism among the populace. Belief in the myths and fantasies regarding the rise and the glory of the Aryan race, embodied in the German nation, masked the reality of the profound immorality of the extermination of the Jews. A number of prominent figures, including 1920s aviation pioneer and American hero Charles Lindbergh, were successfully deceived about the real nature of the Third Reich and its aims. The ideology of racial anti-Semitism wrought unspeakable horror to a population whose only crime was its designation as a dangerous, inferior race.

Even so, the post-Holocaust vow of the Jews of "Never again!" is a cry of resistance that speaks to the indestructible dignity of the Jews. Although we would not like to admit it, the ideology of anti-Semitism remains, in perhaps a subtler, quieter form, even as the smoke of the crematoria has cleared and the death camps have become catacombs for bearing witness. Although the danger of a new strain of the ideology is there, it is the grace of their human dignity that enabled a remnant of Jews to resist by sheer survival to leave an oral and written testimony about the moral evil ordinary human beings are capable of committing. Even though international provisions were made after the Holocaust to try to prevent another occurrence of genocide,[57] at least two genocides, several mass killings, and a number of what have been euphemistically called "ethnic cleansings" have occurred, suggesting that ideologies of death, and the personal and communal foundations for them, have yet to be addressed. In chapter 6, I will discuss the implications, personal and corporate, of acknowledging that human dignity and its defacement are theo-political realities. ▪

Human Dignity and Defacement as Theo-Political Realities

I believe slaveholding to be a sin against God and man.

—HENRY BIBB

Silence is the real crime against humanity.

—SARAH BERKOWITZ

When truly understood, a theological conception of human dignity forces us to renounce all forms of defacement. It calls us to acknowledge and affirm a divine basis for the common bond between us. It gives us a religious basis for cultivating a culture of concern for one another, particularly for the ones who are lodged precariously along the margins. It gives us a basis for challenging the nature of our economic, social, and political systems that hinder our life together. This theological conception of human dignity, rightly understood, leaves us no choice but to recognize that human dignity is indeed a political reality.[1]

In my observation in chapter 2 of human dignity as the glory imparted to us by virtue of God's having created us in the image of God, I suggested that this image renders us of inestimable value in the sight of God. If this is true, and I believe it is, then what God values we must value as well. We are connected to one another not only biologically, as members of the same species, but also theologically, by the imprint of God in each of us. Therefore, we are obligated to manifest this bonded-ness in the context of our economic, social, and political life together. This theological tie should be reflected in the institutions that relate to the making of policy in the societies in which we live.

Our values shape our crucial decisions. They shape decisions as to who is worthy and who is not. They determine whether profit or people come first. They determine whether we focus on the needs of the marginalized or on the wants of the upper and middle class. Our values determine what we will protect at all cost and what we cast aside because it is of low priority. Our values determine who will be given power and authority and how that authority will be used. Our values determine whether we give our allegiance to ideologies or to God. They determine whether decisions are made in which those of privilege or those who are part of our tribe or our nation are valued more than others. Human dignity *is* political.

Every issue that we face can be framed such that affirming or denying the value of human dignity as a political reality can determine whether we are affirming a culture of life or a culture of death. For example, how do we frame our debates about immigration in the United States? What language do we use with respect to those who take extraordinary chances to come here because they, too, want an opportunity to make a better life for *their* families, for *their* children? Regardless of where we stand on this issue, the language—and the spirit *behind* the words used—should raise red flags: "*illegal* immigrants," said as if their aspirations for a better life are somehow different from our own; "illegal *aliens*," pronounced as though somehow they come from another galaxy. Their entry into this country is spoken of as if they are as destructive as a plague of locusts that will render this land barren.

Or, if we take as another example the wars in Afghanistan and Iraq, we can see the ways the value of human dignity does not enter into the equation in terms of whether we will fight, how we will engage in war, and how long we will permit the carnage to continue. Whether we label a war just or unjust, the issue of human dignity remains the same. In *every* war, we are required to label another group the enemy. We will invariably value the lives of some over others. The cries of some mothers, fathers, wives, and children will be felt to be more deep and indicative of suffering than others. As decisions are made about allocating our resources, attention or inattention to human dignity will determine whether we consistently put our resources toward tools of destruction rather than toward constructive engagement with those whom we experience as a problem.

In a theological conception of human dignity, we acknowledge a basis for a common bond between us. We also have a religious foundation for cultivating a culture of concern for one another. We have grounds for challenging the nature of our economic, social, and political systems that hinder the likelihood of a wholesome life together. It is by providing this basic foundation on which we can view our common life that we can say that human dignity is political.

If human dignity is "political," human defacement is no less so. What we learn from hearing the voices of those who told their stories in the slave narratives and the Holocaust survivor memoirs is that their degradation was embedded in the economic, social, and political structures of their oppressors. The genesis of both white supremacy and anti-Semitism reflects that the assault of the dignity of these populations developed into communal dimensions that eventually became structural. If we are to learn anything from these particular histories, which I believe have universal application, then we must acknowledge that both human dignity and human defacement are theo-political realities that demand a total reframing of the way we conduct domestic and international politics.

If we take seriously the witness borne to us through the slave narratives and Holocaust survivor memoirs, then we must be willing to acknowledge that the protection of human dignity demands that we be partisan toward those who are threatened with defacement. If we take seriously the meaning of human dignity, both theologically and politically, we are called on to take sides. Why the insistence on *particular* concern for the marginalized, the poor, and the disinherited? Because of this roll call of names:

. . . Henry Bibb, Sarah Berkowitz, Yitskhok Rudashevski, Malinda Dicus, Sarah Douglass, Etty Hillesum, Jack Maddox, Charles Ball, Miriam Korber, Thomas Cole, Reska Weiss, Olga Lengyel . . .

and all the other men, women, and children who have been mentioned by name in this volume. Those who have been named, and the many, many more who go unnamed, are part of the cloud of witnesses whose testimonies remind all of us what happens when individuals, communities, and nations within the international community choose, for whatever reasons, to remain neutral, uncommitted, or simply uninvolved. If we realize what is truly at stake in the matter of human dignity, we can no longer afford to be indifferent about human defacement. The repeated acts of genocide, and the mass killings that the international community has declined to label "genocide"—*since the Holocaust*—clearly indicate that a commitment to stem the tide of defacement is in order. This form of partisanship must express itself with a sense of great urgency in local, national, and international communities. People are suffering. Children are dying. And the earth is stained with human blood.

African American theologian Howard Thurman—a champion of the defaced, whom he called "the disinherited"—articulated the kind of commitment I believe is called for to staunch the flow of human blood that stains the earth.[2] Thurman saw commitment as a discipline of the body rooted in the determination to live.[3] Because "life is alive," living things continue to survive as long as the vitality, which is life, is available to them.[4] Wherever life is, it is seeking to live out its potential.[5] When the dignity of human beings is denied or assaulted, the quality of all our lives suffers. If we are going to live in a way that supports the vitality needed for each one of us to fulfill our God-given potential, then a commitment must be made by each one of us to safeguard the dignity of all. This commitment must be one in which each one of us yields the deepest recesses of our consent to this purpose.[6] This is a commitment that must be more important than whether individually we live or die in the process of upholding it. This commitment requires a surrender of the very essence of who we are and what we are to this purpose.[7] This commitment must permeate all areas of our lives.

Such a level of commitment requires *conversion*.[8] Conversion, of course, is a theological term. But we have argued that human dignity and human defacement are theological realities as well as political realities. The remedy for defacement must be understood in theological terms as well. Conversion from indifference to defacement involves the recognition of one's alienation from God, the created order (including human beings), and ourselves. It involves a complete reorientation of our priorities. It requires modifying our notions of self-interest. It involves determining the degree to which safeguarding the human dignity of the least valued in our communities becomes the principal value of how we structure our personal and communal lives, and the way in which we develop and maintain policies, systems, and structures to sustain them. This conversion must have not only domestic but also international dimensions. Clearly, the profound changes needed to make the protection of human dignity, especially for the marginalized, a core value requires nothing short of divine grace. We cannot sustain this kind of commitment without it.

While the conversion that leads to commitment is decidedly theological, it is undoubtedly political as well. The conversion of which I speak is clearly not just an individualistic enterprise. The decision to hold or not to hold peoples of African descent was not limited to individual slaveholders. Nor was the decision to participate in the attempt to slaughter European Jews limited to individual Nazi executioners. The sin of defacement in both contexts was individual and communal, with structural embeddedness. Likewise, the sin of defacement in each mass killing and genocide after the Holocaust has also been individual and communal, with structural embeddedness. Therefore, conversion and commit-ment will have to be as broad and wide-ranging as well.

The likelihood of a mass conversion and commitment to safe-guarding the dignity of all, but particularly the least among us, is small. However, the testimony of those who have borne witness compels us to move in this direction. Those who are attuned to what these witnesses are saying to us about ourselves must carry the desire to convert and commit as a driving hunger of the heart. Meanwhile, the testimony of future witnesses will continue to reflect in poignant and graphic detail that the attempt to violate the glory of the human made in the image of God can be seen in their bodies. The human beings we encounter in our daily walk or on the evening news will continue to confront us in the form of the face, with visible, concrete manifestations of their value and worth in the eyes of God. The sacredness that we will see in their faces will say not only, as Emmanuel Levinas asserts, "Thou Shalt not Kill," but also, "You are connected to me."

NOTES

Chapter One: Dignity in the Shadow Side of Human Experience

1. See Simone Weil, "On Human Personality," in *Utopian Pessimist: The Life and Thought of Simone Weil*, ed. David McLellan (New York: Poseidon, 1980), 273–88.

2. The term *Shoah* is another name for the Holocaust.

3. Alexandra Zapruder, ed., *Salvaged Pages: Young Writers' Diaries of the Holocaust* (New Haven, Conn.: Yale University Press, 2002), 23.

4. Zapruder, *Salvaged Pages*, 33.

5. James Mellon, ed., *Bullwhip Days, The Slaves Remember: An Oral History* (New York: Grove, 1988), 240.

6. Mellon, *Bullwhip Days*, 199.

7. Mellon, *Bullwhip Days*, 200.

8. Georg Iggers was a panelist at the symposium "Protesting Prejudice after the Holocaust: The American Experience," which was held on November 3, 2005, at the United States Holocaust Memorial Museum in Washington, D.C.

9. Mellon, *Bullwhip Days*, 29.

10. Mellon, *Bullwhip Days*, 29.

11. Mellon, *Bullwhip Days*, 290.

12. Charles Ball, "Slavery in the United States: A Narrative of the Life and Adventures of Charles Ball, a Black Man, Who Lived Forty Years in Maryland, South Carolina and Georgia as a Slave," in *I Was Born a Slave: An Anthology of Classic Slave Narratives*, vol. 1 (1772–1849), ed. Yuval Taylor (Chicago: Lawrence Hill, 1999), 266.

13. Kate Drumgoold, "A Slave Girl's Story, Being an Autobiography of Kate Drumgoold," in *Six Women's Slave Narratives*, ed. William L. Andrews (New York: Oxford University Press, 1988), 5 (emphasis added).

14. Olga Lengyel, *Five Chimneys* (1947; repr., Chicago: Academy Chicago, 2000), 11.

15. Lengyel, *Five Chimneys*, 24.

16. Aaron Hass, *The Aftermath: Living with the Holocaust* (Cambridge: Cambridge University Press, 1995), 13–14.

17. Primo Levi, *Survival in Auschwitz: The Nazi Assault on Humanity*, trans. Stuart Woolf (New York: Simon & Schuster, 1996), 19.

18. Mellon, *Bullwhip*, 46.

19. Many of the ex-slaves interviewed for *Bullwhip* often referred to themselves and each other as "niggers."

20. Mellon, *Bullwhip*, 219.

21. Lewis Clarke, "Narratives of the Sufferings of Lewis and Milton Clarke, Sons of a Soldier of the Revolution, during a Captivity of More than Twenty Years among the Slaveholders

of Kentucky, One of the So Called Christian States of North America," in Taylor, *I Was Born a Slave*, vol. 1, 618.

22. Clarke, "Lewis and Milton Clarke," 618.

23. Clarke, "Lewis and Milton Clarke," 618.

24. Clarke, "Lewis and Milton Clarke," 660 (emphasis added).

25. Hass, *The Aftermath*, 60.

26. Hass, *The Aftermath*, 12.

27. Lengyel, *Five Chimneys*, 38.

28. Viktor Frankl, *Man's Search for Meaning*, rev. ed. (New York: Simon & Schuster, 1984), 48.

29. Carol Rittner and John K. Roth, eds., *Different Voices: Women and the Holocaust* (St. Paul, Minn.: Paragon, 1993), 111.

30. Mellon, *Bullwhip*, 78.

31. Levi, *Survival in Auschwitz*, 34.

32. Mellon, *Bullwhip*, 291.

33. Mellon, *Bullwhip*, 406.

34. Mellon, *Bullwhip*, 399.

35. Mellon, *Bullwhip*, 401.

36. However, two examples of texts devoted to women and the Holocaust do come to mind: Dalia Ofer and Lenore J. Weitzman, eds., *Women in the Holocaust* (New Haven, Conn.: Yale University Press, 1998), and Rittner and Roth, *Different Voices*.

37. Harriet Jacobs (Linda Brent), "Incidents in the Life of a Slave Girl," in *I Was Born a Slave: An Anthology of Classic Slave Narratives*, vol. 2 (1849–1866), ed. Yuval Taylor (Chicago: Lawrence Hill, 1999), 560.

38. Mellon, *Bullwhip*, 220.

39. Mellon, *Bullwhip*, 296.

40. Hass, *The Aftermath*, 12.

41. Lengyel, *Five Chimneys*, 115.

42. Mellon, *Bullwhip*, 18.

43. Mellon, *Bullwhip*, 18.

44. Mellon, *Bullwhip*, 18.

45. Mellon, *Bullwhip*, 29.

46. Mellon, *Bullwhip*, 210.

47. Mellon, *Bullwhip*, 59 (emphasis added).

48. Hass, *The Aftermath*, xvii.

49. Zapruder, *Salvaged Pages*, 282.

50. Zapruder, *Salvaged Pages*, 203.

51. Zapruder, *Salvaged Pages*, 203.

52. Zapruder, *Salvaged Pages*, 267.

53. Zapruder, *Salvaged Pages*, 107.

54. Zapruder, *Salvaged Pages*, 378.

55. Zapruder, *Salvaged Pages*, 187.

56. Zapruder, *Salvaged Pages*, 187.

57. Ofer and Weitzman, *Women in the Holocaust*, 274.

58. Lengyel, *Five Chimneys*, 16.

59. Lengyel, *Five Chimneys*, 17.

60. Lengyel, *Five Chimneys*, 19.

61. Vincent Harding, *There Is a River: The Black Struggle for Freedom in America* (New York: Harcourt Brace, 1981), 3. See also Marcus Rediker, *The Slave Ship: A Human History* (New York: Viking, 2007), 67–72, 199, 241.

62. Harding, *There Is a River*, 3.

63. Harding, *There Is a River*, 3.

64. Rediker, *The Slave Ship*, 72.

65. Harding, *There Is a River*, 11.

66. Rediker, *The Slave Ship*, 292.

67. Rediker, *The Slave Ship*, 5. Marcus Rediker offers this esti-
    mate, which is close to the estimated number of Jews who died
    during the Holocaust.

68. The exact number of African slaves brought to the New World
    has not been determined, although the estimate of eleven to
    twelve million comes from shipping records from the time.
    Some estimates of the number go as high as thirteen million.
    The editors of *Captive Passage* estimate that about 6 percent of
    the total number of captives arrived in North America. See
    *Captive Passage: The Transatlantic Slave Trade and the Making
    of the Americas* (Washington, D.C.: Smithsonian Institution;
    Newport News, Va.: Mariners' Museum, 2002), 10.

69. This phrase is borrowed from a chapter title in Terrence Des
    Pres, *The Survivor: An Anatomy of Life in the Death Camps*
    (Oxford: Oxford University Press, 1976), 51–71.

70. Ofer and Weitzman, *Women in the Holocaust*, 277.

71. Rittner and Roth, *Different Voices*, 87.

72. Des Pres, *The Survivor*, 58.

73. Des Pres, *The Survivor*, 61.

74. Olaudah Equiano, *The Life of Olaudah Equiano, or Gustavus
    Vassa, the African* (Mineola, N.Y.: Dover, 1999), 33.

75. Des Pres, *The Survivor*, 52.

76. Des Pres, *The Survivor*, 65.

77. Mellon, *Bullwhip*, 60 (emphasis added).

78. Mellon, *Bullwhip*, 185.

79. Mellon, *Bullwhip*, 292.

80. John Brown, "Slave Life in Georgia: A Narrative of the Life, Sufferings, and Escape of John Brown, A Fugitive Slave, Now in England," in Taylor, *I Was Born a Slave*, vol. 2, 363.

81. Mellon, *Bullwhip*, 302.

82. Henry Bibb, "Narrative of the Life and Adventures of Henry Bibb, An American Slave," in Taylor, *I Was Born a Slave*, vol. 2, 19–20.

83. Mellon, *Bullwhip*, 428.

84. Charles Ball, "Slavery in the United States," in Taylor, *I Was Born a Slave*, vol. 1, 275.

85. William Wells Brown, "Narrative of William W. Brown, A Fugitive Slave," in Taylor, *I Was Born a Slave*, vol. 1, 699.

86. Brown, "Narrative of William W. Brown," 706.

87. Brown, "Narrative of William W. Brown," 702. Brown went on to become the first black author to have a novel published. He was also the author of countless documents that railed against the system of slavery.

88. Bibb, "Narrative of the Life and Adventures of Henry Bibb," in Taylor, *I Was Born a Slave*, vol. 2, 15.

89. Mellon, *Bullwhip*, 40.

90. Mellon, *Bullwhip*, 116.

91. Mellon, *Bullwhip*, 456.

92. Hass, *The Aftermath*, 12.

93. Lengyel, *Five Chimneys*, 225.

94. Sarah Bick Berkowitz, *Where Are My Brothers?* (New York: Helios, 1965), 42–43, as quoted in Des Pres, *The Survivor*, 33.

95. Elinor Lipper, *Eleven Years in Soviet Prison Camps*, trans. Richard and Clara Winston (London: World Affairs, 1951; London: Hollis & Carter, 1952), viii, as quoted in Des Pres, *The Survivor*, 37.

96. Nadezhda Mandelstam, *Hope against Hope*, trans. Max Hayward (New York: Atheneum, 1970; London: Harvill, 1971), 379, as quoted in Des Pres, *The Survivor*, 34–35.

97. Lengyel, *Five Chimneys*, 158.

98. Rittner and Roth, *Different Voices*, 111.

99. Hass, *The Aftermath*, xii.

100. Des Pres, *The Survivor*, 31.

101. Hass, *The Aftermath*, xiv.

102. Hass, *The Aftermath*, 60.

103. Bibb, "Narrative of the Life and Adventures of Henry Bibb," in Taylor, *I Was Born a Slave*, vol. 2, 12.

Chapter Two: Human Dignity: The Glory of Humanity

1. Parts of the following discussion appear in Beverly Eileen Mitchell, *Black Abolitionism: The Quest for Human Dignity* (Maryknoll, N.Y.: Orbis, 2005), 4–5. An abridged version also appears in the May/June 2008 issue of the *American Baptist Quarterly*.

2. Reinhold Niebuhr, *The Nature and Destiny of Man*, vol. 1, *Human Nature* (New York: Scribner's Sons, 1964), 167.

3. Niebuhr, The Nature and Destiny of Man, vol. 1, 167.

4. For a more elaborate discussion, see Mitchell, *Black Abolitionism*, 155n3.

5. Niebuhr, *The Nature and Destiny of Man*, vol. 1, 13.

6. Political scientists Robert P. Kraynak and Glenn Tinder demonstrate that there is no consensus among contemporary writers and that the concept of human dignity has changed over the centuries. See Robert P. Kraynak and Glenn Tinder, eds., *In Defense of Human Dignity: Essays for Our Times* (Notre Dame, Ind.: University of Notre Dame Press, 2003).

7. An initial discussion of these elements appears in Mitchell, *Black Abolitionism*, 4–6. See also Robert P. Kraynak, "Made in the Image of God: The Christian View of Human Dignity and Political Order," in Kraynak and Tinder, *In Defense of Human Dignity*, 81–118; Timothy P. Jackson, "A House Divided, Again: Sanctity vs. Dignity in the Induced Death Debates," in Kraynak and Tinder, *In Defense of Human Dignity*, 139–63; Francis Fukuyama, *Our Posthuman Future: Consequences of the Biotechnology Revolution* (New York: Farrar, Straus and Giroux, 2003); and Raimond Gaita, *A Common Humanity: Thinking about Love and Truth and Justice* (London: Routledge, 2000).

8. It is important to note that this dignity is not predicated upon intellectual capacity or physical acuity (or the lack thereof). Thus, not only do infants have this dignity but also the mentally impaired at birth or through disease, the physically impaired, those with congenital defects, and even the dead do. This inclusive understanding of the nature of human dignity precludes futile attempts to procure dignity for ourselves or to seek to deny it to others based on supposed defects. See also Mitchell, *Black Abolitionism*, 155n4.

9. The following discussion is drawn and adapted from Mitchell, *Black Abolitionism*, 4–5. It also appears in the May/June 2008 issue of the *American Baptist Quarterly*. It is based on Gaita, *A Common Humanity*, xx, 82 (emphasis added).

10. Terrence Des Pres, *The Survivor: An Anatomy of Life in the Death Camps* (Oxford: Oxford University Press, 1976), 65–66.

11. From the back cover of Emmanuel Levinas, *Entre Nous: On Thinking-of-the-Other*, trans. Michael B. Smith and Barbara Harshav (New York: Columbia University Press, 1998).

12. Levinas, *Entre Nous*, 169.

13. Levinas, *Entre Nous*, 173.

14. Colin Davis, *Levinas: An Introduction* (Notre Dame, Ind.: University of Notre Dame Press, 1996), 46.

15. Davis, *Levinas*, 135.

16. I prefer not to use the term *structural sin*. I want to acknowledge, emphatically, that the sin of defacement invades structures and systems within societies, but I do not want to obscure the fact that it is *people* who sin, *not* the structures and systems that they develop and for which they are responsible. To speak of "structural" sin is to suggest that structures commit sin. Clearly, this is not the case. Social structures and systems may be demonic or diabolical in the way in which they deface people, but these systems and structures are created by human beings.

17. Kevin Bales has done considerable work in documenting this new form of slavery in the age of globalization. See Kevin Bales, *Disposable People: New Slavery in the Global Economy* (Berkeley, Calif.: University of California Press, 1999).

Chapter Three: Anti-Semitism and Black Antipathy:
Early Patterns of Dehumanization

1. Paul E. Grosser and Edwin G. Halperin, *Anti-Semitism: The Causes and Effects of a Prejudice* (Secaucus, N.J.: Citadel, 1979), 49–50.

2. Kendall Soulen, "God's First Love: Michael Wyschogrod on Israel's Election," *Christian Century*, July 27, 2004, 26.

3. Soulen, "God's First Love," 22.

4. Soulen, "God's First Love," 26.

5. David Novak, "From Supersessionism to Parallelism in Jewish-Christian Dialogue," in *Jews and Christians: People of God*, ed. Carl E. Braaten and Robert W. Jenson (Grand Rapids, Mich.: Eerdmans, 2003), 98.

6. Grosser and Halperin, *Anti-Semitism*, 72.

7. Grosser and Halperin, *Anti-Semitism*, 82.

8. Grosser and Halperin, *Anti-Semitism*, 101. In "On the Governance of Jews (1263)," a response to a letter from a government official, Aquinas writes: "Your Highness asks first: When and where may you exact tribute from the Jews? Put thus in abstract terms, I can only answer that, as the law states, the Jews were, or are, bound to perpetual servitude because of their guilt and as such, rulers may treat their property as their own, albeit with the restriction that the Jews should not be deprived of the necessities of life." See John Hood, *The Essential Aquinas Writings on Philosophy, Religion, and Society* (Westport, Conn.: Praeger, 2002), 210.

9. For example, see Luther's treatise "On the Jews and Their Lies" (1543), in *Luther's Works*, vol. 47, *The Christian in Society, IV*, ed. Franklin Sherman (Philadelphia: Fortress Press, 1971),

121–306. His "advice" on what Christians should do to the Jews, such as set fire to their synagogues, raze their homes, take away their prayer books and Talmudic writings, and so forth, is difficult to comprehend as an appropriate response to religious differences. This is especially true since he had originally resisted the anti-Semitic tendencies of the religious culture of his day. Martin Luther is sometimes cited as the progenitor of modern German anti-Semitism. However repugnant his later writings were with regard to the Jews, the trajectory from his religious anti-Jewish sentiments to the secular, racialized form of National Socialism does not form a *direct* line. Yet, it must be acknowledged that the logic of his ranting in the treatise cited above does raise a valid question as to whether he would have advocated the genocide of the Jews that occurred in the twentieth century.

10. Grosser and Halperin, *Anti-Semitism*, 122.

11. Grosser and Halperin, *Anti-Semitism*, 122.

12. Grosser and Halperin, *Anti-Semitism*, 132.

13. Robert S. Wistrich, *Antisemitism: The Longest Hatred* (New York: Schocken, 1991), 29.

14. Thomas F. Gossett, *Race: The History of an Idea in America* (New York: Schocken, 1963), 16, 17.

15. Gossett, *Race*, 17.

16. Gossett, *Race*, 29.

17. Gossett, *Race*, 30. Gossett notes that Guy B. Johnson maintains that it is doubtful that whites felt the same about blacks as they did toward white bond-servants (see Guy B. Johnson, "Patterns of Race Conflict," in Edgar T. Thompson, ed., *Race Relations and the Race Problem: A Definition and Analysis* [Dur-

ham, N.C.: Duke University Press, 1939], 125–26.) Johnson's observation seems quite plausible.

18. I am indebted to Vincent Harding for this notion of Africans as "chosen" for slavery in the Western Hemisphere. See Vincent Harding, *There Is a River: The Black Struggle for Freedom in America* (New York: Harcourt Brace, 1981), 7–8.

19. See Milton Meltzer, *Slavery: A World History*, updated ed. (New York: Da Capa, 1993), 201–3.

Chapter Four: Racism and Anti-Semitism in Modernity

1. Allen Wood, "The Enlightenment," in *The Encyclopedia of Religion*, vol. 5, ed. Mircea Eliade (New York: Macmillan, 1987), 110.

2. Wood, "The Enlightenment," 109.

3. John Kent, "The Enlightenment," in *The Companion Encyclopedia of Theology*, ed. Peter Byrne and Leslie Houlden (London: Routledge, 1995), 252.

4. Kent, "The Enlightenment," 251.

5. Kent, "The Enlightenment," 256.

6. Kent, "The Enlightenment," 263–64.

7. Gordon G. Brittan Jr., "The Enlightenment," in *The Cambridge Dictionary of Philosophy*, 2nd ed., ed. Robert Audi (Cambridge: Cambridge University Press, 1999), 266.

8. Wood, "The Enlightenment," 113.

9. Kent, "The Enlightenment," 268.

10. Brittan, "The Enlightenment," 266.

11. Peter Gay, *The Enlightenment: The Science of Freedom* (New York: Norton, 1969), 172.

12. Reinhold Niebuhr, *The Nature and Destiny of Man*, vol. 1, *Nature* (New York: Scribner's Sons, 1964), 61.

13. Niebuhr, *The Nature and Destiny of Man*, vol. 1, *Nature*, 64–65.

14. Julie K. Ward and Tommy L. Lott, introduction to *Philosophers on Race: Critical Essays*, ed. Julie K. Ward and Tommy L. Lott (Malden, Mass.: Blackwell, 2002), xi.

15. Cornel West, *Prophesy Deliverance! An Afro-American Revolutionary Christianity* (Philadelphia: Westminster, 1982), 49, 50, 53. Part of this discussion of West also appears in Beverly Eileen Mitchell, *Black Abolitionism: The Quest for Human Dignity* (Maryknoll, N.Y.: Orbis, 2005), 102–3.

16. West, *Prophesy Deliverance!*, 54.

17. West, *Prophesy Deliverance!*, 51.

18. West, *Prophesy Deliverance!*, 65.

19. Thomas F. Gossett, *Race: The History of an Idea in America* (New York: Schocken, 1963), 34.

20. Gossett, *Race*, 34.

21. Gossett, *Race*, 53.

22. Gossett, *Race*, 35.

23. Gossett, *Race*, 35.

24. Gossett, *Race*, 36.

25. Gossett, *Race*, 36.

26. Gossett, *Race*, 36.

27. Gossett, *Race*, 37–39.

28. Gossett, *Race*, 39–40.

29. Gossett, *Race*, 51.

30. Gossett, *Race*, 41–42. Other writers, such as Roger Wilkins in *Jefferson's Pillow: The Founding Fathers and the Dilemma of Black Patriotism* (Boston: Beacon, 2001), and John Hope Franklin in *From Slavery to Freedom: A History of Negro Americans*, 5th ed. (New York: Knopf, 1980), have noted that some of the Founding Fathers felt the discomfort of the contradiction between slaveholding and their gospel of liberty.

31. Thomas Jefferson, *Notes on the State of Virginia* (Chapel Hill, N.C.: University of North Carolina Press, 1955), 138–143. With regard to the political reasons that would preclude successful integration of the races, Jefferson said the following: "It will probably be asked, Why not retain and incorporate the blacks into the state, and thus save the expense of supplying, by importation of white settlers the vacancies they leave? Deep rooted prejudices entertained by the whites; ten thousand recollections, by the blacks, of the injuries they have sustained . . . will divide us into parties, and produce convulsions which will probably never end but in the extermination of the one or the other race." See *Notes on the State of Virginia*, 138.

32. Jefferson, *Notes on the State of Virginia*, 138, 139.

33. This denial of a rich inner life and the capacity to suffer as deeply as whites do is a feature of racism that Raimond Gaita addresses quite pointedly in his discussion of racism as the denial of a common humanity. See Gaita, *A Common Humanity: Thinking about Love and Truth and Justice* (London: Routledge, 2000), 57–72. Here, Jefferson provides the perfect illustration of Gaita's point of view regarding the nature of racism. This is also one of the features of racism that African Americans and other minorities find so infuriating.

34. Jefferson, *Notes on the State of Virginia*, 139, 140. Through his musings, Jefferson seems, on the one hand, to concede that the "difference of condition, of education, of conversation, of the sphere in which they move," might account for the failings that he perceives in the black race. Nevertheless, despite the caution he places on judging blacks, he denigrates them in a way that suggests that he doubted that blacks would ever favorably compare with whites, even if their circumstances changed for the better.

35. Gossett, *Race*, 47–48.

36. Gossett, *Race*, 50.

37. West, *Prophesy Deliverance!*, 61.

38. West, *Prophesy Deliverance!*, 61.

39. West, *Prophesy Deliverance!*, 62.

40. West, *Prophesy Deliverance!*, 62–63.

41. Gossett, *Race*, 51.

42. Lucy S. Dawidowicz, *The War against the Jews, 1933–1945* (New York: Bantam, 1975), 32.

43. Dawidowicz, *The War against the Jews*, 32.

44. The term *anti-Semitism* was first coined by Wilhelm Marr in the 1870s.

45. Paul E. Grosser and Edwin G. Halperin, *Anti-Semitism: The Causes and Effects of a Prejudice* (Secaucus, N.J.: Citadel Press, 1979), 207.

46. Grosser and Halperin, *Anti-Semitism*, 209.

47. I am indebted to J. L. A. Garcia for his definition of racism (see Garcia, "The Heart of Racism," in *Race and Racism*, ed. Bernard Boxill [Oxford: Oxford University Press, 2003], 259).

My definition is similar to his in many respects; however, I have chosen to elaborate on some points in light of the historical experiences of African Americans and European Jews.

48. This definition of racism holds even though ongoing debate that calls into question the reality of a biological concept of race. This definition also applies to anti-Semitism, even though the Jews were originally understood as a religious group rather than an ethnic group, because the Jews have been treated as a racialized caste since the nineteenth century.

Chapter Five: White Supremacy and Racial Anti-Semitism: Ideologies of Death

1. Parts of this discussion on faith and ideology were published in my dissertation: Beverly Eileen Mitchell, *Karl Barth and James Cone: The Question of Liberative Faith and Ideology* (PhD diss., Boston College, 1999).

2. Juan Luis Segundo, *Faith and Ideologies*, trans. John Drury (Maryknoll, N.Y.: Orbis, 1984), 3.

3. Segundo, *Faith and Ideologies*, 28.

4. Juan Luis Segundo, *Liberation of Theology*, trans. John Drury (Maryknoll, N.Y.: Orbis, 1985), 7.

5. Allan Aubrey Boesak, *Farewell to Innocence: A Socio-Ethical Study on Black Theology and Black Power* (Maryknoll, N.Y.: Orbis, 1977), 100.

6. Boesak, *Farewell to Innocence*, 100.

7. Boesak, *Farewell to Innocence*, 101.

8. Boesak, *Farewell to Innocence*, 101.

9. Boesak, *Farewell to Innocence*, 102.

10. Boesak, *Farewell to Innocence*, 102.

11. The notion of faith as *fiducia* or trust has a long history in Christian thought. For example, the sixteenth-century Protestant Reformer Martin Luther often speaks about faith as *fiducia*. For one instance, see his exposition of the letter to the Romans, chapter 8:15–16, in *Luther's Works*, vol. 25, p. 71. Here he maintains that the one who believes with full faith and trusts that one is a child of God is truly a child of God: "Now that you have been freed, you have not received this spirit of fear a second time, but rather the spirit of sonship in trusting faith."

      The theme of faith as *fiducia* is echoed implicitly by sixteenth-century Reformer John Calvin, writing a generation later than Luther. In *The Institutes of the Christian Religion*, bk. 3, ch. 2, para. 7, p. 551, Calvin defines faith as "a firm and certain knowledge of God's benevolence toward us, founded upon the truth of the freely given promise in Christ, both revealed to our minds and sealed upon our hearts through the Holy Spirit."

12. George D. Kelsey defines ethnocentrism as "the belief in the unique value and rightness of one's own group." He concedes that it is "universal" and "perennial." What distinguishes ethnocentrism from racialism, as manifested in white supremacy, is that ethnocentrism is "non-racial" and the distinction with other groups does not seek to keep its "blood" pure. Kelsey maintains that "ethnocentrism is not racial [and therefore not a source of concern] when it is based on religion, culture, class, or shared memories and experience." See Kelsey, *Racism and the Christian Understanding of Man* (1965; repr., Eugene, Ore.: Wipf and Stock, 2001), 19–20.

13. Kelsey, *Racism and the Christian Understanding of Man*, 23.

14. Kelsey, *Racism and the Christian Understanding of Man*, 23.

15. Kelsey, *Racism and the Christian Understanding of Man*, 25.

16. I contend that it is *both*. Racism is a theological error because it impugns the character of God in terms of the good creation and it invariably leads one to value something (for example, one's racial classification) more than God. Racism is an anthropological error because it leads one to violate the commandment to love one's neighbor as oneself. This commandment cannot be kept if one does not value and respect the other person as equally a child of God.

17. Kelsey, *Racism and the Christian Understanding of Man*, 26.

18. In several places in *Racism and the Christian Understanding of Man*, Kelsey draws parallels between the treatment and experience of blacks and Jews with regard to racialism. One example of a sustained, though brief, discussion of the Jews and anti-Semitism can be found on pages 63–66.

19. Kelsey, *Racism and the Christian Understanding of Man*, 29 (emphasis added).

20. See Lucy S. Dawidowicz, *The War against the Jews, 1933–1945* (New York: Bantam, 1975), 27. Dawidowicz's discussion is based on historian George L. Mosse, *Toward the Final Solution: A History of European Racism* (New York: Fertig, 1978).

21. Robert P. Ericksen, *Theologians under Hitler: Gerhard Kittel, Paul Althaus and Emanuel Hirsch* (New Haven, Conn.: Yale University Press, 1985), 103; quoted from Paul Althaus, *Volker vor und nach Christus* (Leipzig, 1937), 7.

22. Ericksen, *Theologians under Hitler*, 103; quoted from Althaus, *Volker vor und nach Christus*, 8.

23. Dawidowicz, *The War against the Jews*, 28.

24. Dawidowicz, *The War against the Jews*, 28.

25. Dawidowicz, *The War against the Jews*, 29.

26. John Hope Franklin, *From Slavery to Freedom: A History of Negro Americans*, 5th ed. (New York: Knopf, 1980), 134–35, 136.

27. C. Vann Woodward, "Folkways, Stateways, and Racism," in *The Strange Career of Jim Crow*, reprinted in *The Segregation Era, 1863–1954: A Modern Reader*, ed. Allen Weinstein and Frank Otto Gatell (New York: Oxford University Press, 1970), 73.

28. Woodward, "Folkways, Stateways, and Racism," 77.

29. Woodward, "Folkways, Stateways, and Racism," 79.

30. Woodward, "Folkways, Stateways, and Racism," 81.

31. Eric Foner, *Reconstruction: America's Unfinished Revolution, 1863–1877* (New York: Harper & Row, 1988), 425.

32. Sanford Wexler, *An Eyewitness History of the Civil Rights Movement* (New York: Checkmark, 1993), 4.

33. Wexler, *An Eyewitness History of the Civil Rights Movement*, 5.

34. Wexler, *An Eyewitness History of the Civil Rights Movement*, 5.

35. Wexler, *An Eyewitness History of the Civil Rights Movement*, 5–6.

36. Wexler, *An Eyewitness History of the Civil Rights Movement*, 1, 2, 13.

37. Aldon D. Morris, *The Origins of the Civil Rights Movement: Black Communities Organizing for Change* (New York: Free Press, 1984), 1–3.

38. Here we might recall the almost hysterical opposition to intimate social interaction between black males and white females, with the possibilities of mixed-race children. The intimate

relationship, at least openly or publicly, between white males and black females was far more complex. Although it was viewed negatively, black females were always vulnerable to sexual exploitation at the hands of white males.

39. Dawidowicz, *The War against the Jews*, 58–59.

40. Dawidowicz, *The War against the Jews*, 59.

41. Dawidowicz, *The War against the Jews*, 59. The definition of a non-Aryan calls to mind the standards applied with regard to who was black in the United States—that is, one drop of "black blood" rendered one black.

42. Dawidowicz, *The War against the Jews*, 63.

43. Dawidowicz, *The War against the Jews*, 65.

44. Dawidowicz, *The War against the Jews*, 65.

45. Dawidowicz, *The War against the Jews*, 69.

46. Robert S. Wistrich, *Anti-Semitism: The Longest Hatred* (New York: Schocken, 1994), 73.

47. Marion A. Kaplan, *Between Dignity and Despair: Jewish Life in Nazi Germany* (New York: Oxford University Press, 1998), 121–22.

48. Kaplan, *Between Dignity and Despair*, 119.

49. Wistrich, *Anti-Semitism*, 73.

50. The SS began as an armed formation within the SA (Sturm-abteilung) to protect the führer, top party leaders, and party meetings. They became an important instrument of the "final solution." See Dawidowicz, *The War against the Jews*, 70–87.

51. Wistrich, *Anti-Semitism*, 73.

52. Kaplan, *Between Dignity and Despair*, 119.

53. Dawidowicz, *The War against the Jews*, 121.

54. Dawidowicz, *The War against the Jews*, 140.

55. Dawidowicz, *The War against the Jews*, 147.

56. Dawidowicz, *The War against the Jews*, 148. Although most of the victims of the death camps were Jews, Gypsies and thousands of non-Jews were also gassed.

57. The Universal Declaration of Human Rights was established in 1945 as a direct result of the atrocities of the Nazi regime.

58. The two genocides occurred in Rwanda and Darfur; the ethnic cleansing, in the Bosnian conflict; and the killing fields, in Cambodia under the Khmer Rouge regime.

Chapter Six: Human Dignity and Defacement as Theo-Political Realities

1. The discussion of human dignity as a theo-political reality was initially discussed in my inaugural lecture (February 21, 2008) and appears in the Summer 2008 edition of the *American Baptist Quarterly*. This current chapter expands on that discussion to also include the concept of human defacement as a theo-political reality.

2. This discussion of commitment and conversion draws from and is inspired by Howard Thurman's book *Disciplines of the Spirit* (Richmond, Ind.: Friends United, 1987).

3. Thurman, *Disciplines of the Spirit*, 13.

4. Thurman, *Disciplines of the Spirit*, 14,

5. Thurman, *Disciplines of the Spirit*, 15.

6. Thurman, *Disciplines of the Spirit*, 17.

7. Thurman, *Disciplines of the Spirit*, 19.

8. The concept of conversion in this discussion is inspired by Thurman's discussion of the connection between commitment and conversion in relation to disciplines of the Spirit. See Thurman, *Disciplines of the Spirit*, 23–26.

BIBLIOGRAPHY

Andrews, William L., ed. *Six Women's Slave Narratives*. Oxford: Oxford University Press, 1988.

Aquinas, Thomas. "On the Governance of Jews." In *The Essential Aquinas Writings on Philosophy, Religion, and Society*, edited by John Hood, 210–11. Westport, Conn.: Praeger, 2002.

Bales, Kevin. *Disposable People: New Slavery in the Global Economy*. Berkeley, Calif.: University of California Press, 1999.

Boesak, Allan Aubrey. *Farewell to Innocence: A Socio-Ethical Study on Black Theology and Black Power*. Maryknoll, N.Y.: Orbis, 1977.

Brittan, Gordon G., Jr. "The Enlightenment." In *The Cambridge Dictionary of Philosophy*, 2nd ed., edited by Robert Audi. Cambridge: Cambridge University Press, 1999.

Calvin, John. *The Institutes of the Christian Religion*. Edited by John T. McNeill. Philadelphia: Westminster, 1960.

Captive Passage: The Transatlantic Slave Trade and the Making of the Americas. Washington, D.C.: Smithsonian Institution Press; Newport News, Va.: Mariners' Museum, 2002.

Davis, Colin. *Levinas: An Introduction*. Notre Dame, Ind.: University of Notre Dame Press, 1996.

Dawidowicz, Lucy S. *The War against the Jews, 1933–1945*. New York: Bantam, 1975.

Des Pres, Terrence. *The Survivor: An Anatomy of Life in the Death Camps*. Oxford: Oxford University Press, 1976.

Dillenberger, John, ed. *Martin Luther: Selections from His Writings*. Garden City, N.Y.: Anchor, 1961.

Equiano, Olaudah. *The Life of Olaudah Equiano, or Gustavus Vassa, the African*. Mineola, N.Y.: Dover, 1991.

Ericksen, Robert P. *Theologians under Hitler: Gerhard Kittel, Paul Althaus and Emanuel Hirsch*. New Haven, Conn.: Yale University Press, 1985.

Foner, Eric. *Reconstruction: America's Unfinished Revolution, 1863–1877*. New York: HarperCollins, 1988.

Frankl, Viktor E. *Man's Search for Meaning*. Rev. ed. Boston: Simon & Schuster, 1984.

Franklin, John Hope. *From Slavery to Freedom: A History of Negro Americans*. 5th ed. New York: Knopf, 1980.

Fukuyama, Francis. *Our Posthuman Future: Consequences of the Biotechnology Revolution*. New York: Farrar, Straus and Giroux, 2003.

Gaita, Raimond. *A Common Humanity: Thinking about Love and Truth and Justice*. London: Routledge, 2000.

Garcia, J. L. A. "The Heart of Racism." In *Race and Racism*, edited by Bernard Boxill, 256–96. Oxford: Oxford University Press, 2003.

Gay, Peter. *The Enlightenment: The Science of Freedom*. New York: Norton, 1969.

Gossett, Thomas F. *Race: The History of an Idea in America*. Dallas: Southern Methodist University Press, 1963.

Grosser, Paul E., and Edwin G. Halperin. *Anti-Semitism: The Causes and Effects of a Prejudice*. Secaucus, N.J.: Citadel Press, 1979.

Harding, Vincent. *There Is a River: The Black Struggle for Freedom in America*. San Diego, Calif.: Harcourt Brace, 1981.

Hass, Aaron. *The Aftermath: Living with the Holocaust*. Cambridge: Cambridge University Press, 1995.

Hood, John. *The Essential Aquinas Writings on Philosophy, Religion, and Society*. Westport, Conn.: Praeger, 2002.

Jefferson, Thomas. *Notes on the State of Virginia*. Chapel Hill, N.C.: University of North Carolina, 1955.

Kaplan, Marion A. *Between Dignity and Despair: Jewish Life in Nazi Germany*. New York: Oxford University Press, 1998.

Kelsey, George D. *Racism and the Christian Understanding of Man*. 1965. Reprint, Eugene, Ore.: Wipf and Stock, 2001.

Kent, John. "The Enlightenment." In *Companion Encyclopedia of Theology*, edited by Peter Byrne and Leslie Houlden, 251–268. London: Routledge, 1995.

Kraynak, Robert P., and Glenn Tinder, eds. *In Defense of Human Dignity: Essays for Our Time*. Notre Dame, Ind.: University of Notre Dame Press, 2003.

Lengyel, Olga. *Five Chimneys: A Woman Survivor's True Story of Auschwitz*. 1947. Reprint, Chicago: Academy Chicago, 2000.

Levi, Primo. *Survival in Auschwitz: The Assault on Humanity*. Translated by Stuart Woolf. New York: Touchstone, 1996.

Levinas, Emmanuel. *Entre Nous: On Thinking-of-the Other.* Translated by Michael B. Smith and Barbara Harshav. New York: Columbia University Press, 1998.

Luther, Martin. "Lectures on Romans." Chap. 8 in *Luther's Works,* vol. 25, edited by Hilton C. Oswald. Saint Louis, Mo.: Concordia, 1972.

———. "On the Jews and Their Lies." In *Luther's Works,* vol. 47, *The Christian in Society IV,* edited by Franklin Sherman. Philadelphia: Fortress, 1971.

Mellon, James, ed. *Bullwhip Days, The Slaves Remember: An Oral History.* New York: Grove, 1988.

Meltzer, Milton. *Slavery: A World History.* Updated ed. New York: Da Capo, 1993.

Mitchell, Beverly Eileen. *Black Abolitionism: A Quest for Human Dignity.* Maryknoll, N.Y.: Orbis, 2005.

———. *Karl Barth and James Cone: The Question of Liberative Faith and Ideology.* PhD diss., Boston College, 1999.

Morris, Aldon D. *The Origins of the Civil Rights Movement: Black Communities Organizing for Change.* New York: Free Press, 1984.

Mosse, George L. *Toward the Final Solution: A History of European Racism.* New York: Fertig, 1978.

Niebuhr, Reinhold. *Moral Man, Immoral Society.* New York: Scribner's Sons, 1960.

———. *The Nature and Destiny of Man.* Vol. 1, *Human Nature.* New York: Scribner's Sons, 1964.

Novak, David. "From Supersessionism to Parallelism in Jewish-Christian Dialogue." In *Jews and Christians: People of God.* Grand Rapids, Mich.: Eerdmans, 2003.

Ofer, Dalia, and Lenore J. Weitzman. *Women in the Holocaust*. New Haven, Conn.: Yale University Press, 1998.

Rediker, Marcus. *The Slave Ship: A Human History*. New York: Viking, 2007.

Rittner, Carol, and John K. Roth, eds. *Different Voices: Women and the Holocaust*. St. Paul, Minn.: Paragon House, 1993.

Segundo, Juan Luis. *Faith and Ideologies*. Translated by John Drury. Maryknoll, N.Y.: Orbis, 1984.

———. *Liberation of Theology*. Translated by John Drury. Maryknoll, N.Y.: Orbis, 1985.

Soulen, Kendall. "God's First Love: Michael Wyschogrod on Israel's Election." *Christian Century*, July 27, 2004.

Taylor, Yuval, ed. *I Was Born a Slave: An Anthology of Classic Slave Narratives*. Vol. 1 (1772–1849). Chicago: Lawrence Hill, 1999.

———. *I Was Born a Slave: An Anthology of Classic Slave Narratives*. Vol. 2 (1849–1866). Chicago: Lawrence Hill, 1999.

Thurman, Howard. *Disciplines of the Spirit*. Richmond, Ind.: Friends United, 1977; 2nd ed., 1987.

Ward, Julia K., and Tommy L. Lott. *Philosophers on Race: Critical Essays*. Oxford: Blackwell, 2002.

Weil, Simone. "On the Human Personality." Appendix. In *Utopian Pessimist: The Life and Thought of Simone Weil*, by David McLellan. New York: Poseidon, 1990.

———. *Waiting for God*. 1951. Reprint, Harper & Row, 1973.

West, Cornel. *Prophesy Deliverance! An Afro-American Revolutionary Christianity*. Philadelphia: Westminster, 1982.

Wexler, Sanford. *An Eyewitness History of the Civil Rights Movement*. New York: Checkmark, 1993.

Wilkins, Roger. *Jefferson's Pillow: The Founding Fathers and the Dilemma of Black Patriotism*. Boston: Beacon, 2001.

Wistrich, Robert S. *Antisemitism: The Longest Hatred*. New York: Schocken, 1991.

Wood, Allen. "The Enlightenment." In *The Encyclopedia of Religion*, vol. 5, edited by Mircea Eliade, 109–13. New York: Macmillan, 1987.

Woodward, C. Vann. "Folkways, Stateways, and Racism." In *The Strange Career of Jim Crow*. Reprinted in *The Segregation Era, 1863–1954: A Modern Reader*, by Allen Weinstein and Frank Otto Gatell. New York: Oxford University Press, 1970.

Zapruder, Alexandra, ed. *Salvaged Pages: Young Writers' Diaries of the Holocaust*. New Haven, Conn.: Yale University Press, 2002.

INDEX

CPSIA information can be obtained
at www.ICGtesting.com
Printed in the USA
LVHW010412090821
694848LV00012B/1170

9 780800 663308